PENGUIN BOOKS

RELIGION FOR ATHEISTS

Alain de Botton was born in 1969 and is the author of non-fiction essays on themes ranging from love and travel to architecture and philosophy. His bestselling books include *How Proust Can Change Your Life*, *The Art of Travel* and *The Architecture of Happiness*. He lives in London and founded The School of Life (www.theschooloflife.com) and Living Architecture (www. living-architecture.co.uk).

w.alaindebotton.com

I2514617

Religion for Atheists

*A non-believer's guide
to the uses of religion*

Alain de Botton

PENGUIN BOOKS

PENGUIN BOOKS

Published by the Penguin Group
Penguin Books Ltd, 80 Strand, London WC2R 0RL, England
Penguin Group (USA) Inc., 375 Hudson Street, New York, New York 10014, USA
Penguin Group (Canada), 90 Eglinton Avenue East, Suite 700, Toronto, Ontario, Canada M4P 2Y3
(a division of Pearson Penguin Canada Inc.)
Penguin Ireland, 25 St Stephen's Green, Dublin 2, Ireland
(a division of Penguin Books Ltd)
Penguin Group (Australia), 250 Camberwell Road,
Camberwell, Victoria 3124, Australia (a division of Pearson Australia Group Pty Ltd)
Penguin Books India Pvt Ltd, 11 Community Centre,
Panchsheel Park, New Delhi – 110 017, India
Penguin Group (NZ), 67 Apollo Drive, Rosedale, Auckland 0632, New Zealand
(a division of Pearson New Zealand Ltd)
Penguin Books (South Africa) (Pty) Ltd, Block D, Rosebank Office Park,
181 Jan Smuts Avenue, Parktown North, Gauteng 2193, South Africa

Penguin Books Ltd, Registered Offices: 80 Strand, London WC2R 0RL, England

www.penguin.com

First published by Hamish Hamilton 2012
Published in Penguin Books 2012
002

Typeset in ITC Galliard by April
Printed in Finland by Bookwell Ltd

ISBN: 978–0–141–04631–0
Export edition ISBN: 978–0–241–96405–7

MIX
Paper from
responsible sources
FSC   FSC™ C018179
www.fsc.org

For Bertha von Büren

Contents

I

Wisdom without Doctrine

Probably just a very nice person: St Agnes of Montepulciano.

1.

The most boring and unproductive question one can ask of any religion is whether or not it is *true* – in terms of being handed down from heaven to the sound of trumpets and supernaturally governed by prophets and celestial beings.

To save time, and at the risk of losing readers painfully early on in this project, let us bluntly state that of course no religions are true in any God-given sense. This is a book for people who are unable to believe in miracles, spirits or tales of burning shrubbery, and have no deep interest in the exploits of unusual men and women like the thirteenth-century saint Agnes of Montepulciano, who was said to be able to levitate two feet off the ground while praying and to bring children back from the dead – and who, at the end of her life (supposedly), ascended to heaven from southern Tuscany on the back of an angel.

2.

Attempting to prove the non-existence of God can be an entertaining activity for atheists. Tough-minded critics of religion have found much pleasure in laying bare the idiocy of believers in remorseless detail, finishing only when they felt they had shown up their enemies as thorough-going simpletons or maniacs.

Though this exercise has its satisfactions, the real issue is not whether God exists or not, but where to take the argument once one decides that he evidently doesn't. The premise of this book is that it must be possible to remain a committed atheist and nevertheless find religions sporadically useful, interesting and consoling – and be curious as to the possibilities of importing certain of their ideas and practices into the secular realm.

One can be left cold by the doctrines of the Christian Trinity and the Buddhist Eightfold Path and yet at the same time be interested in the ways in which religions deliver sermons, promote morality, engender a spirit of community, make use of art and architecture, inspire travels, train minds and encourage gratitude at the beauty of spring. In a world beset by fundamentalists of both believing and secular varieties, it must be possible to balance a rejection of religious faith with a selective reverence for religious rituals and concepts.

It is when we stop believing that religions have been handed down from above or else that they are entirely daft that matters become more interesting. We can then recognize that we invented religions to serve two central needs which continue to this day and which secular society has not been able to solve with any particular skill: first, the need to live together in communities in harmony, despite our deeply rooted selfish and violent impulses. And second, the need to cope with terrifying degrees of pain which arise from our vulnerability to professional failure, to troubled relationships, to the death of loved ones and to our decay and demise. God may be dead, but the urgent issues which impelled us to make him up still stir and demand resolutions which do not go away when we have been nudged to perceive some scientific inaccuracies in the tale of the seven loaves and fishes.

The error of modern atheism has been to overlook how many aspects of the faiths remain relevant even after their central tenets have been dismissed. Once we cease to feel that we must either prostrate ourselves before them or denigrate them, we are free to discover religions as repositories of a myriad ingenious concepts with which we can try to assuage a few of the most persistent and unattended ills of secular life.

3.

I was brought up in a committedly atheistic household, as the son of two secular Jews who placed religious belief somewhere on a par with an attachment to Santa Claus. I recall my father reducing my sister to tears in an attempt to dislodge her modestly held notion that a reclusive god might dwell somewhere in the universe. She was eight years old at the time. If any members of their social circle were discovered to harbour clandestine religious sentiments, my parents would start to regard them with the sort of pity more commonly reserved for those diagnosed with a degenerative disease and could from then on never be persuaded to take them seriously again.

Though I was powerfully swayed by my parents' attitudes, in my mid-twenties I underwent a crisis of faithlessness. My feelings of doubt had their origins in listening to Bach's cantatas, were further developed in the presence of certain Bellini Madonnas and became overwhelming with an introduction to Zen architecture. However, it was not until my father had been dead for several years – and buried under a Hebrew headstone in a Jewish cemetery in Willesden, north-west London, because he had, intriguingly, omitted to make more secular arrangements – that I began to face up to the full scale of my ambivalence regarding the doctrinaire principles with which I had been inculcated in childhood.

I never wavered in my certainty that God did not exist. I was simply liberated by the thought that there might be a way to engage with religion without having to subscribe to its super-natural content – a way, to put it in more abstract terms, to think about Fathers without upsetting my respectful memory of my own father. I recognized that my continuing resistance to theo-ries of an afterlife or of heavenly residents was no justification for giving up on the music, buildings, prayers, rituals, feasts, shrines, pilgrimages, communal meals and illuminated manuscripts of the faiths.

Secular society has been unfairly impoverished by the loss of an array of practices and themes which atheists typically find it impossible to live with because they seem too closely associated with, to quote Nietzsche's useful phrase, 'the bad odours of religion'. We have grown frightened of the word *morality*. We bridle at the thought of hearing a sermon. We flee from the idea that art should be uplifting or have an ethical mission. We don't go on pilgrimages. We can't build temples. We have no mechanisms for expressing gratitude. The notion of reading a self-help book has become absurd to the high-minded. We resist mental exercises. Strangers rarely sing together. We are presented with an unpleasant choice between either committing to peculiar concepts about imma-terial deities or letting go entirely of a host of consoling, subtle or just charming rituals for which we struggle to find equivalents in secular society.

In giving up on so much, we have allowed religion to claim as its exclusive dominion areas of experience which should rightly belong to all mankind – and which we should feel unembarrassed about reappropriating for the secular realm. Early Christianity was itself highly adept at appropriating the good ideas of others, aggressively subsuming countless pagan practices which modern atheists now tend to avoid in the mistaken belief that they are indelibly Christian. The new faith took over celebrations of midwinter and repackaged them as Christmas. It absorbed the Epicurean ideal of living together in a philosophical community and turned it into what we now know as monasticism. And in the ruined cities of the old Roman Empire, it blithely inserted itself into the empty shells of temples once devoted to pagan heroes and themes.

The challenge facing atheists is how to reverse the process of religious colonization: how to separate ideas and rituals from the religious institutions which have laid claim to them but don't truly own them. For instance, much of what is best about Christmas is entirely unrelated to the story of the birth of Christ. It revolves around themes of community, festivity and renewal which pre-date the context in which they were cast over the centuries by Christianity. Our soul-related needs are ready to be freed of the particular tint given to them by religions – even if it is, paradoxically, the study of religions which often holds the key to their rediscovery and rearticulation.

What follows is an attempt to read the faiths, primarily Christianity and to a lesser extent Judaism and Buddhism, in

Religions have a habit of squatting on things which did not originally belong to them, as seen here in the Church of San Lorenzo in Miranda, Rome, built in the seventeenth century within the remains of the Roman temple of Antoninus and Faustina.

the hope of gleaning insights which might be of use within secular life, particularly in relation to the challenges of community and of mental and bodily suffering. The underlying thesis is not that secularism is wrong, but that we have too often secularized badly – inasmuch as, in the course of ridding ourselves of unfeasible ideas, we have unnecessarily surrendered some of the most useful and attractive parts of the faiths.

4.

The strategy outlined in this book will, of course, annoy partisans on both sides of the debate. The religious will take offence at a seemingly brusque, selective and unsystematic consideration of their creeds. Religions are not buffets, they will protest, from which choice elements can be selected on a whim. However, the downfall of many a faith has been its unreasonable insistence that adherents must eat everything on the plate. Why should it not be possible to appreciate the depiction of modesty in Giotto's frescoes and yet bypass the doctrine of the annunciation, or to admire the Buddhist emphasis on compassion and yet shun its theories of the afterlife? For someone devoid of religious belief, it may be no more of a crime to borrow from a number of faiths than it is for a lover of literature to single out a handful of favourite writers from across the canon. If mention is made here of only three of the world's twenty-one largest religions, it is no sign of favouritism or impatience, just a consequence of the way that the emphasis of this book lies on comparing religion in general with the secular realm, rather than on comparing an array of religions with one another.

Atheists of the militant kind may also feel outraged, in their case by a book that treats religion as though it deserves to be a continuing touchstone for our yearnings. They will point to the furious institutional intolerance of many religions, and to the equally rich, though less illogical and illiberal, stores of consolation and insight available through art and science. They may additionally ask why anyone who professes himself unwilling to accept so many facets of religion – who feels unable to speak up in the name of virgin births, say, or to nod at the claims reverently made in the Jataka tales about the Buddha's identity as a reincarnated rabbit – should still wish to associate himself with a subject as compromised as faith.

To this the answer is that religions merit our attention for their sheer conceptual ambition; for changing the world in a way that few secular institutions ever have. They have managed to combine theories about ethics and metaphysics with a practical involvement in education, fashion, politics, travel, hostelry, initiation ceremonies, publishing, art and architecture – a range of interests which puts to shame the scope of the achievements of even the greatest and most influential secular movements and individuals in history. For those interested in the spread and impact of ideas, it is hard not to be mesmerized by examples of the most successful educational and intellectual movements the planet has ever witnessed.

5.

To conclude, this book does not endeavour to do justice to particular religions; they have their own apologists. It tries, instead, to examine aspects of religious life which contain concepts that could fruitfully be applied to the problems of secular society. It attempts to burn off religions' more dogmatic aspects in order to distil a few aspects of them that could prove timely and consoling to sceptical contemporary minds facing the crises and griefs of finite existence on a troubled planet. It hopes to rescue some of what is beautiful, touching and wise from all that no longer seems true.

II

Community

i. Meeting Strangers

1.

One of the losses modern society feels most keenly is that of a sense of community. We tend to imagine that there once existed a degree of neighbourliness which has been replaced by ruthless anonymity, a state where people pursue contact with one another primarily for restricted, individualistic ends: for financial gain, social advancement or romantic love.

Some of our nostalgia centres around our reluctance to give charitably to others in distress, but we are as likely to be concerned with pettier symptoms of social separation, our failure to say hello to one another in the street, for instance, or to help elderly neighbours with the shopping. Living in gargantuan cities, we tend to be imprisoned within tribal ghettos based on education, class and profession and may come to view the rest of humanity as an enemy rather than as a sympathetic collective we would aspire to join. It can be extraordinary and odd to start an impromptu conversation with an unknown person in a public space. Once we are past the age of thirty, it is even somewhat surprising to make a new friend.

In attempting to understand what could have eroded our sense of community, an important role has traditionally been accorded to the privatization of religious belief that occurred in Europe and the United States in the nineteenth century. Historians have suggested that we began to disregard our neighbours at around the same time as we ceased communally to honour our gods. This begs the question of what religions

might have done, prior to that time, to enhance the spirit of community, and, more practically, whether secular society could ever recover this spirit without relying on the theological superstructure with which it was once entwined. Could it be possible to reclaim a sense of community without having to base it on religious foundations?

2.

If we examine the causes of modern alienation in more detail, some of our sense of loneliness comes down to sheer numbers. The billions of people who live on the planet make the idea of talking to a stranger more threatening than it was in sparser days, because sociability seems to bear an inverse relationship to the density of population. We generally talk gladly to people only once we also have the option of avoiding them altogether. Whereas the Bedouin whose tent surveys a hundred kilometres of desolate sand has the psychological wherewithal to offer each stranger a warm welcome, his urban contemporaries, though at heart no less well meaning or generous, must – in order to preserve a modicum of inner serenity – give no sign of even noticing the millions of humans who are eating, sleeping, arguing, copulating and dying only centimetres away from them on all sides.

Then, too, there is the matter of how we are introduced. The public spaces in which we typically encounter others – the commuter trains, the jostling pavements, the airport concourses – conspire to project a demeaning picture of our identities, which undermines our capacity to hold on to the idea that every person is necessarily the centre of a complex and precious individuality. It can be hard to stay hopeful about human nature after a walk down Oxford Street or a transfer at O'Hare.

We used to feel more connected to our neighbours in part because they were also often our colleagues. Home was not always an anonymous dormitory to be reached late and left early. Neighbours became well acquainted not so much because they were adept conversationalists, but because they had to bring in the hay or put up the school roof together, such projects naturally and surreptitiously helping to foster connections. However, capitalism has little patience for local production and cottage industry. It may even prefer it if we have no contact with our neighbours at all, lest they detain us on our way to the office or discourage us from completing an online acquisition.

In the past, we got to know others because we had no option but to ask them for help – and were ourselves asked for help in turn. Charity was an integral part of premodern life. It was impossible to avoid moments when we would have to request money from a near-stranger or to hand it out to a vagabond beggar in a world without a health-care system, unemployment insurance, public housing or consumer banking. The approach on the street of a sick, frail, confused or homeless person did not immediately inspire passers-by to look away and assume that a government agency would take care of the problem.

We are from a purely financial point of view greatly more generous than our ancestors ever were, surrendering up to half of our income for the communal good. But we do this almost without realizing it, through the anonymous agency of the taxation system; and if we think about it at all, it is likely to be with resentment that our money is being used to support unnecessary bureaucracies or to buy missiles. We seldom feel a connection to those less fortunate members of the polity for whom our taxes also buy clean sheets, soup, shelter or a daily dose of insulin. Neither recipient nor donor feels the need to say 'Please' or 'Thank you'. Our donations are never framed – as they were in the Christian era – as the lifeblood of an intricate tangle of mutually interdependent relationships, with practical benefits for the recipient and spiritual ones for the donor.

Locked away in our private cocoons, our chief way of imagining what other people are like has become the media, and as a consequence, we naturally expect that all strangers will be murderers, swindlers or paedophiles – which reinforces our impulse to trust only those few individuals who have been vetted for us by pre-existing family and class networks. On those rare occasions when circumstances (snowstorms, lightning strikes) succeed in rupturing our hermetic bubbles and throw us in with people we don't know, we tend to marvel that our fellow citizens have shown surprisingly little interest in slicing us in half or molesting our children and may even be surprisingly good-natured and ready to help.

Solitary though we may have become, we haven't of course given up all hope of forming relationships. In the lonely canyons of the modern city, there is no more honoured emotion than love. However, this is not the love of which religions speak, not the expansive, universal brotherhood of mankind, it is a more

Dreams of meeting one person who will spare us any need for other people.

jealous, restricted and ultimately meaner variety. It is a romantic love which sends us on a maniacal quest for a single person with whom we hope to achieve a life-long and complete communion, one person in particular who will spare us any need for people in general.

In so far as modern society ever promises us access to a community, it is one centred around the worship of professional success. We sense that we are brushing up against its gates when the first question we are asked at a party is 'What do you do?', our answer to which will determine whether we are warmly welcomed or conclusively abandoned by the peanuts. In these competitive, pseudo-communal gatherings, only a few of our attributes count as currency with which to buy the goodwill of strangers. What matters above all is what is on our business cards, and those who have opted to spend their lives looking after children, writing poetry or nurturing orchards will be left in no doubt that they have run contrary to the dominant mores of the powerful and deserve to be marginalized accordingly.

Given this level of discrimination, it is no surprise that many of us choose to throw ourselves with a vengeance into our careers. Focusing on work to the exclusion of almost everything else is a plausible enough strategy in a world which accepts workplace achievements as the main tokens with which we can secure not just the financial means to survive physically, but also the attention that we require to thrive psychologically.

3.

Religions seem to know a great deal about our loneliness. Even if we believe very little of what they tell us about the afterlife or the supernatural origins of their doctrines, we can nevertheless admire their understanding of what separates us from strangers and their attempts to melt away one or two of the prejudices that normally prevent us from building connections with others.

A Catholic Mass is not, to be sure, the ideal habitat for an atheist. Much of the dialogue is either offensive to reason or simply incomprehensible. It goes on for a long time and rarely overrides a temptation to fall asleep. Nevertheless, the ceremony is replete with elements which subtly strengthen congregants' bonds of affection, and which atheists would do well to study and on occasion learn to appropriate for reuse in the secular realm.

Catholicism starts to create a sense of community with a setting. It marks off a piece of the earth, puts walls up around it and declares that within their parameters there will reign values utterly unlike those which hold sway in the world beyond, in the offices, gyms and living rooms of the city. All buildings give their owners opportunities to recondition visitors' expectations and to lay down rules of conduct specific to them. The art gallery legitimates the practice of peering silently at a canvas, the nightclub of swaying one's hands to a musical score. And a church, with its massive timber doors and 300 stone angels carved around its porch, gives us rare permission to lean over and say hello to a stranger without any danger of being thought predatory or insane. We are promised that here (in the words

of the Mass's initial greeting) 'the love of God and the fellowship of the Holy Spirit' belong to all who have assembled. The Church lends its enormous prestige, accrued through age, learning and architectural grandeur, to our shy desire to open ourselves to someone new.

The composition of the congregation feels significant. Those in attendance tend not to be uniformly of the same age, race, profession or educational or income level; they are a random sampling of souls united only by their shared commitment to certain values. The Mass actively breaks down the economic and status subgroups within which we normally operate, casting us into a wider sea of humanity.

In this secular age, we often assume that a love of family and a sense of community must be synonymous. When modern politicians speak of their wish to repair society, it is the family they hail as the quintessential symbol of community. But Christianity is wiser and less sentimental in this regard, for it acknowledges that an attachment to family may in fact narrow the circle of our affections, distracting us from the greater challenge of apprehending our connection with all of mankind; of learning to love kith as well as kin.

With similarly communal ends in mind, the Church asks us to leave behind all attachments to earthly status. It is the inner values of love and charity rather than the outer attributes of power and money that are now venerated. Among Christianity's greatest achievements has been its capacity, without the use of any coercion beyond the gentlest of theological arguments, to persuade monarchs and magnates to kneel down and abase themselves before the statue of a carpenter, and to wash the feet of peasants, street sweepers and dispatch drivers.

The Church does more, however, than merely declare that worldly success doesn't matter: in a variety of ways, it enables us to imagine that we could be happy without it. Appreciating the reasons why we try to acquire status in the first place, the Church establishes conditions under which we can willingly surrender our attachment to class and titles. It seems to know that we strive to be powerful chiefly because we are afraid of what will happen to us without high rank: we risk being stripped of dignity, being patronized, lacking friends and having to spend our days in coarse and dispiriting surroundings.

It is the genius of the Mass to correct each of these fears in turn. The building in which it is performed is almost always sumptuous. Though it is technically devoted to celebrating the equality of man, it generally surpasses palaces in its beauty. The company is also enticing. We develop a desire to be famous and powerful when being 'like everyone else' seems a distressing fate, when the norm is mediocre and depressing. High status then becomes a tool to separate us from a group we resent and are scared of. However, as the congregants in a cathedral start to sing *Gloria in Excelsis*, we tend to feel that the crowd is nothing like the one we encountered in the shopping malls or the degraded transport hubs outside. Strangers gaze up at the vaulted, star-studded ceiling, rehearse in unison the words

> 'Lord,
> come, live in your people
> and strengthen them by your grace'

and leave us thinking that humanity may not be such a wretched thing after all.

As a result, we may start to feel that we could work a little less feverishly, because we see that the respect and security we hope to gain through our careers is already available to us in a warm and impressive community which imposes no worldly requirements on us for its welcome.

If there are so many references in the Mass to poverty, sadness, failure and loss, it is because the Church views the ill, the frail of mind, the desperate and the elderly as representing aspects of humanity and (even more meaningfully) of ourselves which we are tempted to deny, but which bring us, when we can acknowledge them, closer to our need for one another.

In our more arrogant moments, the sin of pride – or *superbia,* in Augustine's Latin formulation – takes over our personalities and shuts us off from those around us. We become dull to others when all we seek to do is assert how well things are going for us, just as friendship has a chance to grow only when we dare to share what we are afraid of and regret. The rest is merely showmanship. The Mass encourages this sloughing off of pride. The flaws whose exposure we so dread, the indiscretions we know we would be mocked for, the secrets that keep our conversations with our so-called friends superficial and inert – all of these emerge as simply part of the human condition. We have no reason left to dissemble or lie in a building dedicated to honouring the terror and weakness of a man who was nothing like the usual heroes of antiquity, nothing like the fierce soldiers of Rome's army or the plutocrats of its Senate,

and yet who was nevertheless worthy of being crowned the highest of men, the king of kings.

4.

If we have managed to remain awake to (and for) the lessons of the Mass, it should by its close have succeeded in shifting us at least fractionally off our accustomed egocentric axes. It should also have given us a few ideas which we could use to mend some of the endemic fractures of the modern world.

One of the first of these ideas relates to the benefit of taking people into a distinct venue which ought itself to be attractive enough to evoke enthusiasm for the notion of a group. It should inspire visitors to suspend their customary frightened egoism in favour of a joyful immersion in a collective spirit – an unlikely scenario in the majority of modern community centres, whose appearance paradoxically serves to confirm the inadvisability of joining anything communal.

Secondly, the Mass embodies a lesson about the importance of putting forward rules to direct people in their interactions with one another. The liturgical complexity of a missal – the directive way in which this book of instructions for the celebration of a Mass compels the congregants to look up, stand, kneel, sing, pray, drink and eat at given points – speaks to an essential aspect of human nature which benefits from being guided in how to behave with others. To ensure that profound and dignified personal bonds can be forged, a tightly choreographed agenda of activities may be more effective than leaving a group to mingle aimlessly on its own.

S. Osténde nobis Dómine, misericórdiam tuam.
M. *Et salutáre tuum da nobis.*
S. Dómine, exáudi oratiónem meam.
M. *Et clamor meus ad te véniat.*
S. Dóminus vobíscum.
M. *Et cum spíritu tuo.*
S. Orémus.

4. The Priest goes up to the Altar

With a prayer for pardon on his lips the Priest goes up to the Altar which he kisses. He kisses the Altar nine times during the Mass begging for the intercession of the Saints whose relics repose in the altar stone.

First extending, then joining his hands, the Priest says inaudibly OREMUS; *then ascending to the Altar, he says secretly:*

AUFER a nobis, quæsumus Dómine, iniquitátes nostras: ut ad Sancta sanctórum puris mereámur méntibus introíre. Per Christum Dóminum nostrum. Amen.

His hands joined, and bowing down over the Altar, the Priest says:

ORÁMUS te, Dómine, per mérita Sanctórum tuórum, quórum relíquiæ hic sunt, et ómnium Sanctórum: ut indulgére dignéris ómnia peccáta mea. Amen.

In SOLEMN MASSES *the Altar is here incensed. Whilst blessing the incense the Priest says:*

AB illo ✠ benedicáris, in cujus honóre cremáberis. Amen.

P. Show us, O Lord, Thy mercy.

S. *And grant us Thy salvation.*
P. O Lord, hear my prayers.
S. *And let my cry come unto Thee.*
P. The Lord be with you.
S. *And with thy spirit.*
P. Let us pray.

4. The Priest goes up to the Altar

With a prayer for pardon on his lips the Priest goes up to the Altar which he kisses. He kisses the Altar nine times during the Mass begging for the intercession of the Saints whose relics repose in the altar stone.

First extending, then joining his hands, the Priest says audibly OREMUS; *then ascending to the Altar, he says secretly:*

TAKE away from us our iniquities, we beseech Thee, O Lord, that we may be worthy to enter with pure minds into the Holy of Holies: through Christ our Lord. Amen.

His hands joined, and bowing down over the Altar, the Priest says:

WE beseech Thee, O Lord, by the merits of Thy Saints, whose relics are here, and of all the Saints, that Thou wouldst vouchsafe to forgive me all my sins. Amen.

In SOLEMN MASSES *the Altar is here incensed. Whilst blessing the incense the Priest says:*

BE blessed ✠ by Him in whose honour thou art burnt. Amen.

An artificial construct can nevertheless open the door to sincere feelings: rules for how to conduct a Mass, Latin and English instructions from the Roman Missal, 1962.

A final lesson to be taken away from the Mass is closely connected with its history. Before it was a service, before the congregants sat in seats facing an altar behind which a priest held up a wafer and a cup of wine, the Mass was a meal. What we now know as the Eucharist began as an occasion when early Christian communities put aside their work and domestic obligations and gathered together around a table (usually laden with wine, lamb and loaves of unleavened bread) in order to commemorate the Last Supper. There they would talk, pray and renew their commitments to Christ and to one another. Like the Jews with their Sabbath meal, Christians understood that it is when we satiate our bodily hunger that we are often readiest to direct our minds to the needs of others. In honour of the most important Christian virtue, these gatherings hence became known as *agape* (meaning 'love' in Greek) *feasts* and were regularly held by Christian communities in the period between Jesus's death and the Council of Laodicea in AD 364. It was only complaints about the excessive exuberance of some of these meals that eventually led the early Church to the regrettable decision to ban agape feasts and suggest that the faithful should eat at home with their families instead – and only thereafter gather for the spiritual banquet that we know today as the Eucharist.

Before it was a service, the Mass was a meal.

5.

It feels relevant to talk of meals because our modern lack of a proper sense of community is importantly reflected in the way we eat. The contemporary world is not, of course, lacking in places where we can dine well in company – cities typically pride themselves on the sheer number and quality of their restaurants – but what is significant is the almost universal lack of venues that help us to transform strangers into friends.

While contemporary restaurants pay lip service to the notion of companionability, they provide us with only its most inadequate simulacrum. The number of people who nightly patronize restaurants implies that these places must be refuges from anonymity and coldness, but in fact they have no systematic mechanisms by which to introduce patrons to one another, to dispel their mutual suspicions, to break up the clans into which people chronically segregate themselves or to get them to open up their hearts and share their vulnerabilities with others. The focus is on the food and the decor, never on opportunities for extending and deepening affections. In a restaurant no less than in a home, when the meal itself – the texture of the escalopes or the moistness of the courgettes – has become the main attraction, we can be sure that something has gone awry.

Patrons will tend to leave restaurants much as they entered them, the experience having merely reaffirmed existing tribal divisions. Like so many institutions in the modern city, restaurants are adept at gathering people into the same space and yet lack any means of encouraging them to make meaningful contact with one another once they are there.

The food was not the most important thing: Duccio di Buoninsegna,
The Last Supper, 1311.

6.

With the benefits of the Mass and the drawbacks of contemporary dining in mind, we can imagine an ideal restaurant of the future, an Agape Restaurant, true to the most profound insights of the Eucharist.

Such a restaurant would have an open door, a modest entrance fee and an attractively designed interior. In its seating arrangements, the groups and ethnicities into which we commonly segregate ourselves would be broken up; family members and couples would be spaced apart, and kith favoured over kin. Everyone would be safe to approach and address, without fear of rebuff or reproach. By simple virtue of occupying the same space, guests would – as in a church – be signalling their allegiance to a spirit of community and friendship.

Sitting down at a table with a group of strangers has the incomparable and odd benefit of making it a little more difficult to hate them with impunity. Prejudice and ethnic strife feed off abstraction. However, the proximity required by a meal – something about handing dishes around, unfurling napkins at the same moment, even asking a stranger to pass the salt – disrupts our ability to cling to the belief that the outsiders who wear unusual clothes and speak in distinctive accents deserve to be sent home or assaulted. For all the large-scale political solutions which have been proposed to salve ethnic conflict, there are few more effective ways to promote tolerance between suspicious neighbours than to force them to eat supper together.

Many religions are aware that the moments around the ingestion of food are propitious to moral education. It is as if the imminent prospect of something to eat seduces our normally resistant selves into showing some of the same generosity to others as the table has shown to us. These religions also know enough about our sensory, non-intellectual dimensions to be aware that we cannot be kept on a virtuous track simply through the medium of words. They know that at a meal they will have a captive audience who are likely to accept a trade-off between ideas and nourishment – and so they turn meals into disguised ethical lessons. They stop us just before we have a first sip of wine and offer us a thought that can be swilled down with the liquid like a tablet. They make us listen to a homily in the gratified interval between two courses. And they use specific types of food and drink to represent abstract concepts, telling Christians, for example, that bread stands for the sacred body of Christ, informing Jews that the Passover dish of crushed apples and nuts is the mortar used by their enslaved predecessors to build the warehouses of Egypt and teaching Zen Buddhists that their cups of slowly brewing tea are tokens of the transitory nature of happiness in a floating world.

Taking their seats at an Agape Restaurant, guests would find in front of them guidebooks somewhat reminiscent of the Jewish Haggadah or the Catholic missal, laying out the rules for how to behave at the meal. No one would be left alone to find their way to an interesting conversation with another, any more than it would be expected of participants at a Jewish Passover meal or in the Christian Eucharist that they might

An Agape Restaurant, a secular descendant of the Eucharist and of the tradition of Christian communal dining.

manage independently to alight on the salient aspects of the history of the tribes of Israel or achieve a sense of communion with God.

The Book of Agape would direct diners to speak to one another for prescribed lengths of time on predefined topics. Like the famous questions which the youngest child present is assigned by the Haggadah to ask during the Passover ceremony ('Why is this night different from all other nights?', 'Why do we eat unleavened bread and bitter herbs?' and so on), these talking points would be carefully crafted for a specific purpose, to coax guests away from customary expressions of *superbia* ('What do you do?', 'Where do your children go to school?') and towards a more sincere revelation of themselves ('What do you regret?', 'Whom can you not forgive?', 'What do you fear?'). The liturgy would, as in the Mass, inspire charity in the deepest sense, a capacity to respond with complexity and compassion to the existence of our fellow creatures.

One would be privy to accounts of fear, guilt, rage, melancholy, unrequited love and infidelity that would generate an impression of our collective insanity and endearing fragility. Our conversations would free us from some of our more distorted fantasies about others' lives, by revealing the extent to which, behind our well-defended façades, most of us are going a little out of our minds – and so have reason to stretch out a hand to our equally tortured neighbours.

For new participants, the formality of the dinner-time liturgy would no doubt at first seem peculiar. Yet they would gradually appreciate the debt that authentic emotion owes to

We benefit from having books that tell us how to behave at meals. Here, a Haggadah from Barcelona (*c.* 1350), an instruction manual for a precisely choreographed Passover meal, designed to convey a lesson in Jewish history while reanimating a sense of community.

well-judged rules of conduct. After all, it is hardly natural to kneel down with a group of people on a stone floor, to gaze towards an altar and to intone together:

> 'Lord,
>
> we pray for your people who believe in you.
>
> May they enjoy the gift of your love,
>
> share it with others,
>
> and spread it everywhere.
>
> We ask this in the name of Jesus the Lord.
>
> Amen'

– and yet the faithful who attend a Mass do not hold such structured commands against their religion; instead, they welcome them for generating a level of spiritual intensity that would be impossible to summon up in a more casual context.

Thanks to the Agape Restaurant, our fear of strangers would recede. The poor would eat with the rich, the black with the white, the orthodox with the secular, the bipolar with the balanced, workers with managers, scientists with artists. The claustrophobic pressure to derive all of our satisfactions from our existing relationships would ease, as would our desire to gain status by accessing so-called elite circles.

The notion that we could mend some of the tatters in the modern social fabric through an initiative as modest as a communal meal will seem offensive to those with greater trust in the power of legislative and political solutions to cure society's ills. Yet these restaurants would not be an alternative to traditional political methods. They would be a prior step taken to humanize one another in our imaginations, in order that we would

A Passover meal: social mechanisms are at work here that are as useful and complex as those in a parliament or a law court.

then more naturally engage with our communities and, unbidden, cede some of our impulses towards the egoism, racism, aggression, fear and guilt which lie at the root of so many of the issues with which traditional politics is concerned.

Christianity, Judaism and Buddhism have all made significant contributions to mainstream politics, but their relevance to the problems of community are arguably never greater than when they depart from the modern political script and remind us that there is also value to be had in standing in a hall with a hundred acquaintances and singing a hymn together or in ceremoniously washing a stranger's feet or in sitting at a table with neighbours and partaking of lamb stew and conversation, the kinds of rituals which, as much as the deliberations inside parliaments and law courts, are what help to hold our fractious and fragile societies together.

Dressed in traditional white, Israeli Jews walk down a traffic-free road in Jerusalem on their way to attend synagogue on the Day of Atonement.

ii. Apologies

1.

The effort of religions to inspire a sense of community does not stop at introducing us to one other. Religions have also been clever at solving some of what goes wrong inside groups once they are formed.

It has been the particular insight of Judaism to focus on anger: how easy it is to feel it, how hard it is to express it and how frightening and awkward it is to appease it in others. We can see this especially clearly in the Jewish Day of Atonement, one of the most psychologically effective mechanisms ever devised for the resolution of social conflict.

Falling on the tenth day of Tishrei, shortly after the beginning of the Jewish new year, the Day of Atonement (or Yom Kippur) is a solemn and critical event in the Hebrew calendar. Leviticus instructs that on this date, Jews must set aside their usual domestic and commercial activities and mentally review their actions over the preceding year, identifying all those whom they have hurt or behaved unjustly towards. Together in synagogue, they must repeat in prayer:

> 'We have sinned, we have acted treacherously,
> we have robbed, we have spoken slander.
> We have acted perversely, we have acted wickedly,
> we have acted presumptuously, we have been violent,
> we have framed lies.'

They must then seek out those whom they have frustrated, angered, discarded casually or otherwise betrayed and offer

It was no one's idea in particular to say sorry: Yom Kippur Service,
Budapest synagogue.

them their fullest contrition. This is God's will, and a rare opportunity for blanket forgiveness. 'All the people are in fault,' says the evening prayer, and so 'may all the people of Israel be forgiven, including all the strangers who live in their midst'.

On this holy day, Jews are advised to contact their colleagues, sit down with their parents and children and send letters to acquaintances, lovers and ex-friends overseas, and to catalogue their relevant moments of sin. In turn, those to whom they apologize are urged to recognize the sincerity and effort which the offender has invested in asking for their forgiveness. Rather than let annoyance and bitterness towards their petitioner well up in them once more, they must be ready to draw a line under past incidents, aware that their own lives have surely also not been free of fault.

God enjoys a privileged role in this cycle of apology: he is the only perfect being and therefore the only one to whom the need to apologize is alien. As for everyone else, imperfection is embedded in human nature and therefore so too must be the will to contrition. Asking others for forgiveness with courage and honesty signals an understanding of, and respect for, the difference between the human and the divine.

The Day of Atonement has the immense advantage of making the idea of saying sorry look like it came from somewhere else, the initiative of neither the perpetrator nor the victim. It is the day itself that is making us sit here and talk about the peculiar incident six months ago when you lied and I blustered and you accused me of insincerity and I made you cry, an incident that neither of us can quite forget but that we can't quite mention either and which has been slowly corroding the trust and love we once had for each other. It is the day that has given us the opportunity, indeed the responsibility, to stop talking of our usual business and to reopen a case we pretended to have put out of our minds. We are not satisfying ourselves, we are obeying the rules.

2.

The prescriptions of the Day of Atonement bring comfort to both parties to an injury. As victims of hurt, we frequently don't bring up what ails us, because so many wounds look absurd in the light of day. It appalls our reason to face up to how much we suffer from the missing invitation or the unanswered letter, how many hours of torment we have given to the unkind remark or the forgotten birthday, when we should long ago have become serene and impervious to such needles. Our vulnerability insults our self-conception; we are in pain and at the same time offended that we could so easily be so. Our reserve may also have a financial edge. Those who caused us injury are liable to have authority over us – they own the business and decide on the contracts – and it is this imbalance of power that is keeping us quiet, yet not for that matter saving us from bitterness and suppressed rage.

Alternatively, when we are the ones who have caused someone else pain and yet failed to offer apology, it was perhaps because acting badly made us feel intolerably guilty. We can be so sorry that we find ourselves incapable of saying sorry. We run away from our victims and act with strange rudeness towards them, not because we aren't bothered by what we did, but because what we did makes us feel uncomfortable with an unmanageable intensity. Our victims hence have to suffer not only the original hurt, but also the subsequent coldness we display towards them on account of our tormented consciences.

3.

All this the Day of Atonement will help to correct. A period in which human error is proclaimed as a general truth makes it easier to confess to specific infractions. It is more bearable to own up to our follies when the highest authority has told us that we are all childishly yet forgivably demented to begin with.

So cathartic is the Day of Atonement, it seems a pity that there should be only one of them a year. A secular world could without fear of excess adopt its own version to mark the start of every quarter.

iii. Our Hatred of Community

1.

It would be naive to suppose that the only reason we fail to create strong communities is because we are too shy to say hello to others. Some of our social alienation comes down to the many facets of our nature that have no interest whatsoever in communal values, sides that are bored or revolted by fidelity, self-sacrifice and empathy and which instead incline with abandon towards narcissism, jealousy, spite, promiscuity and wanton aggression.

Religions know full well about these tendencies and recognize that if communities are to function, they must be dealt with, but by being artfully purged and exorcized rather than simply repressed. Religions therefore present us with an array of rituals, many of them oddly elaborate at first glance, whose function is to safely discharge what is vicious, destructive or nihilistic in our natures. These rituals don't of course advertise their brief, for to do so would bring a degree of self-consciousness that might make participants flee from them in horror, but their longevity and popularity prove that something vital has been achieved through them.

The best communal rituals effectively mediate between the needs of the individual and those of the group. Expressed freely, certain of our impulses would irreparably fracture our societies. Yet if they were simply repressed with equal force, they would end up challenging the sanity of individuals. The ritual hence conciliates self and others. It is a controlled and often aesthetically moving purgation. It demarcates a space in which our egocentric demands can be honoured and at the same time tamed, in order that the longer-term harmony and survival of the group can be negotiated and assured.

2.

We see some of this at work in the Jewish rituals attendant on the death of a beloved family member. Here the danger is that the mourner will be so overwhelmed with grief that he will cease to assume his responsibilities vis-à-vis the community. The group is therefore given instructions to allow the bereaved fulsome opportunity to express his sadness and yet it also applies a gentle and ever-increasing pressure to make sure that he eventually gets back to the business of living.

In the seven days of *shiva* that follow the funeral, there is allowance for a period of cataclysmic confusion, then a more restrained thirty-day period (*shloshim*) in which one is absolved from many group responsibilities, followed by a whole twelve months (*shneim asar chodesh*) in which the memory of the deceased is commemorated in a mourner's prayer during synagogue services. But at the end of the year, after the unveiling of the headstone (*matzevah*), further prayers, another service and a gathering at home, the claims of life and the community are definitively reasserted.

3.

Funerals aside, most religious communal rituals display outward cheer. They take place in halls with mountains of food, dancing, exchanges of gifts, toasts and an atmosphere

How can sadness be expressed without becoming all-consuming? The impulse might be to give up on life and the community altogether. The unveiling of a Jewish headstone a year after a father's death.

of levity. But beneath the gaiety, there is often also a kernel of sadness in the people at the centre of the ritual, for they are likely to be surrendering a particular advantage for the sake of the community as a whole. The ritual is in truth a form of compensation, a transformational moment when depletion can be digested and sweetened.

It is hard to attend most wedding parties without realizing that these celebrations are at some level also marking a sorrow, the entombment of sexual liberty and individual curiosity for the sake of children and social stability, with compensation from the community being delivered through gifts and speeches.

The Jewish Bar Mitzvah ceremony is another ostensibly joyful ritual which endeavours to assuage inner tensions. Although apparently concerned with celebrating the moment when a Jewish boy enters adulthood, it is as much focused on trying to reconcile his parents to his evolving maturity. The parents are liable to be nursing complex regrets that the nurturing period which began with their son's birth is drawing to a close and – especially in the case of the father – that they will soon have to grapple with their own decline and with a sense of envy and resentment at being equalled and superseded by a new generation. On the day of the ceremony, mother and father are heartily congratulated on the eloquence and accomplishment of their child even as they are also gently encouraged to begin to let him go.

Religions are wise in not expecting us to deal with all of our emotions on our own. They know how confusing and humiliating it can be to have to admit to despair, lust, envy or

Would we ever need ritual festivities if there wasn't also something to be
sad about? A Bar Mitzvah ceremony, New York State.

egomania. They understand the difficulty we have in finding a way to tell our mother unaided that we are furious with her or our child that we envy him or our prospective spouse that the idea of marriage alarms as much as it delights us. They hence give us special days under the cover of which our pestiferous feelings can be processed. They give us lines to recite and songs to sing while they carry us across the treacherous regions of our psyches.

In essence, religions understand that to belong to a community is both very desirable and not very easy. In this respect, they are greatly more sophisticated than those secular political theorists who write lyrically about the loss of a sense of community, while refusing to acknowledge the inherently dark aspects of social life. Religions teach us to be polite, to honour one another, to be faithful and sober, but they also know that if they do not allow us to be or do otherwise every once in a while, they will break our spirit. In their most sophisticated moments, religions accept the debt that goodness, faith and sweetness owe to their opposites.

4.

Medieval Christianity certainly understood this dichotomy. For most of the year, it preached solemnity, order, restraint, fellowship, earnestness, a love of God and sexual decorum, and then on New Year's Eve it opened the locks on the collective psyche and unleashed the *festum fatuorum*, the Feast of Fools. For four days, the world was turned on its head: members of the clergy would play dice on top of the altar, bray like donkeys

To stay sane, we may need an occasional moment to deliver a sermon according to Luke's Toenail. A nineteenth-century illustration of the medieval Feast of Fools.

instead of saying 'Amen', engage in drinking competitions in the nave, fart in accompaniment to the Ave Maria and deliver spoof sermons based on parodies of the gospels (the Gospel according to the Chicken's Arse, the Gospel according to Luke's Toenail). After drinking tankards of ale, they would hold their holy books upside down, address prayers to vegetables and urinate out of bell towers. They 'married' donkeys, tied giant woollen penises to their tunics and endeavoured to have sex with anyone of any gender who would have them.

But none of this was considered just a joke. It was sacred, a *parodia sacra*, designed to ensure that all the rest of the year things would remain the right way up. In 1445, the Paris Faculty of Theology explained to the bishops of France that the Feast of Fools was a necessary event in the Christian calendar, 'in order that foolishness, which is our second nature and is inherent in man, can freely spend itself at least once a year. Wine barrels burst if from time to time we do not open them and let in some air. All of us men are barrels poorly put together, and this is why we permit folly on certain days: so that we may in the end return with greater zeal to the service of God.'

The moral we should draw is that if we want well-functioning communities, we cannot be naive about our nature. We must fully accept the depths of our destructive, antisocial feelings. We shouldn't banish feasting and debauchery to the margins, to be mopped up by the police and frowned upon by commentators. We should give chaos pride of place once a year or so, designating occasions on which we can be briefly exempted from the two greatest pressures of secular adult life: having to be rational and having to be faithful. We should be allowed to talk gibberish, fasten woollen penises to our coats and set out into the night to party and copulate randomly and joyfully with strangers, and then return the next morning to our partners, who will themselves have been off doing something similar, both sides knowing that it was nothing personal, that it was the Feast of Fools that made them do it.

5.

We learn from religion not only about the charms of community. We learn also that a good community accepts just how much there is in us that doesn't really want community – or at least can't tolerate it in its ordered forms all the time. If we have our feasts of love, we must also have our feasts of fools.

Yearly moment of release at the Agape Restaurant.

III

Kindness

i. Libertarianism and Paternalism

1.

Once we are grown up, we are seldom encouraged officially to be nice to one another. A key assumption of modern Western political thinking is that we should be left alone to live as we like without being nagged, without fear of moral judgement and without being subject to the whims of authority. Freedom has become our supreme political virtue. It is not thought to be the state's task to promote a vision of how we should act towards one another or to send us to hear lectures about chivalry and politeness. Modern politics, on both left and right, is dominated by what we can call a libertarian ideology.

In his *On Liberty* of 1859, John Stuart Mill, one of the earliest and most articulate advocates of this hands-off approach, explained: 'The only purpose for which power can be rightfully exercised over any member of a civilized community, against his will, is to prevent harm to others. His own good, either physical or moral, is not sufficient warrant.'

In this scheme, the state should harbour no aspirations to tinker with the inner well-being or outward manners of its members. The foibles of citizens are placed beyond comment or criticism – for fear of turning government into that most reviled and unpalatable kind of authority in libertarian eyes, the nanny state.

2.

Religions, on the other hand, have always had far more directive ambitions, advancing far-reaching ideas about how members of a community should behave towards one another.

Consider Judaism, for example. Certain passages in the Jewish legal code, the Mishnah, have close parallels in modern law. There are familiar-sounding statutes about not stealing, breaking contracts or exacting disproportionate revenge on enemies during war.

However, a great many other decrees extend their reach dramatically far beyond what a libertarian political ideology would judge to be appropriate bounds. The code is obsessed with the details of how we should behave with our families, our colleagues, strangers and even animals. It dictates that we must never sit down to eat a meal before we have fed our goats and our camels, that we should ask our parents for permission when agreeing to go on a journey of more than one night's duration, that we should invite any widows in our communities for dinner every spring-time and that we should beat our olive trees only once during the harvest so as to leave any remaining fruit to the fatherless and to the poor. Such recommendations are capped by injunctions on how often to have sex, with men told of their duty before God to make love to their wives regularly, according to a timetable that aligns frequency with the scale of their professional commitments: 'For men of independent means, every day. For labourers, twice a week. For donkey drivers, once a week. For camel drivers, once in thirty days. For sailors, once every six months' (Mishnah, Ketubot, 5:6).

The Jewish legal code advises not only that stealing is wrong but also that a donkey driver ought to have sex with his wife once a week. Moses receives the Tablets of the Law, from a French Bible, *c.* 834.

3.

Libertarian theorists would concede that it is no doubt admirable to try to satisfy a spouse's sexual needs, to be generous with olives and to keep one's elders abreast of one's travel plans. However, they would also condemn as peculiar and plain sinister any paternalistic attempt to convert these aspirations into statutes. When to feed the dog and ask widows over for supper are, according to a libertarian worldview, questions for the conscience of the individual rather than the judgement of the community.

In secular society, by the libertarian's reckoning, a firm line should divide conduct that is subject to law from conduct that is subject to personal morality. It should fall to parliaments, police forces, courts and prisons to prevent harm to a citizen's life or property – but more ambiguous varieties of mischief should remain within the exclusive province of conscience. Thus the stealing of an ox is a matter to be investigated by a police officer, whereas the oppression of someone's spirit through two decades of indifference in the bedroom is not.

This reluctance to get involved in private matters is rooted less in indifference than in scepticism, and more specifically in a pervasive doubt that anyone could ever be in a position to know exactly what virtue is, let alone how it might be safely and judiciously instilled in others. Aware of the inherent complexity of ethical choices, libertarians cannot fail to notice how few issues fall cleanly into unassailable categories of right and wrong. What may seem like obvious truths to one party can be seen by another as culturally biased prejudices. Looking back upon centuries of religious self-assurance, libertarians stand transfixed by the dangers of conviction. An abhorrence of crude moralism has banished talk of morality from the public sphere. The impulse to question the behaviour of others trembles before the likely answer: who are you to tell me what to do?

4.

However, there is one arena in which we spontaneously favour moralistic intervention over neutrality, an arena which for many of us dominates our practical lives and dwarfs all other concerns in terms of its value: the business of raising our children.

To be a parent is inevitably to mediate forcefully in the lives of one's offspring in the hope that they will some day grow up to be not only law-abiding but also *nice* – that is, thoughtful with their partners, generous-spirited towards the fatherless, self-conscious about their motives and uninclined to wallow in sloth or self-pity. In their length and intensity, parents' admonishments rival those laid out in the Jewish Mishnah.

Faced with the same two questions which so trouble libertarian theorists in the political sphere – 'Who are you to tell me what to do?' and 'How do you know what is right?' – parents have little difficulty in arriving at workable answers. Even as they frustrate their children's immediate wishes (often to the sound of ear-splitting screams), they tend to feel sure that they are guiding them to act in accordance with norms which they would willingly respect if only they were capable of fully developed reason and self-control.

The fact that such parents favour paternalism in their own homes does not mean that they have cast all their ethical doubts aside. They would argue that it is eminently reasonable to be unsure about certain large issues – whether foetuses should ever be aborted beyond twenty-four weeks, for example – while remaining supremely confident about many smaller ones, such as whether it is right to hit one's younger brother in the face or to squirt apple juice across the bedroom ceiling.

To lend concrete form to their pronouncements, parents are often moved to draw up star charts, complex domestic political settlements (usually to be found fastened to the sides of fridges or the doors of larders) which set forth in exhaustive detail the specific behaviours they expect from, and will reward in, their children.

Noting the considerable behavioural improvements these charts tend to produce (along with the paradoxical satisfaction that children appear to derive from having their more disorderly impulses monitored and curtailed), libertarian adults may be tempted to suggest, with a modest laugh at such a palpably absurd idea, that they themselves might benefit from having a star chart pinned to the wall to keep track of their own eccentricities.

5.

If the idea of an adult star chart seems odd but not wholly without merit, it is because we are aware, in our more mature moments, of the scale of our imperfections and the depths of our childishness. There is so much that we would like to do but never end up doing and so many ways of behaving that we subscribe to in our hearts but ignore in our day-to-day lives. However, in a world obsessed with freedom, there are few voices left that ever dare to exhort us to act well.

	m	t	w	t	f	s	s
not hitting Saul in the stomach		⭐			⭐		
saying Thank you to granny	⭐						
eating up vegetables			⭐		⭐		
helping put away all the toys - even Saul's	⭐			⭐		⭐	
not pulling Scratty's tail	⭐						
sharing chocolate treats						⭐	
washing hands after going to the loo		⭐	⭐		⭐		
not peeking during hide and seek			⭐				
not having a tantrum when losing a game - to anyone					⭐		

Even the most theoretically libertarian of parents tend to acknowledge the point of star charts when dealing with four-year-olds.

The exhortations we would need are typically not very complex: forgive others, be slow to anger, dare to imagine things from another's point of view, set your dramas in perspective ... We are holding to an unhelpfully sophisticated view of ourselves if we think that we are always above hearing well-placed, blunt and simply structured reminders about kindness. There is greater wisdom in accepting that we are in most situations rather simple entities in want of much the same kind, firm, basic guidance as is naturally offered to children and domestic animals.

The true risks to our chances of flourishing are different from those conceived of by libertarians. A lack of freedom is no longer, in most developed societies, the problem. Our downfall lies in our inability to make the most of the freedom that our ancestors painfully secured for us over three centuries. We have grown sick from being left to do as we please without sufficient wisdom to exploit our liberty. It is not primarily the case that we find ourselves at the mercy of paternalistic authorities whose claims we resent and want to be free of. The danger runs in an opposite direction: we face temptations which we revile in those interludes when we can attain a sufficient distance from them, but which we lack any encouragement to resist, much to our eventual self-disgust and disappointment. The mature sides of us watch in despair as the infantile aspects of us trample upon our more elevated principles and ignore what we most fervently revere. Our deepest wish may be that someone would come along and save us from ourselves.

An occasional paternalistic reminder to behave well does not have to constitute an infringement of our 'liberty' as this term should properly be understood. Real freedom does not mean being left wholly to one's own devices; it should be compatible with being harnessed and guided.

Modern marriages are a test case of the problems created by an absence of a moral atmosphere. We start off with the best of intentions and a maximal degree of communal support. All eyes are upon us: family, friends and employees of the state appear to be fully invested in our mutual happiness and good behaviour. But soon enough we find ourselves alone with our wedding gifts and our conflicted natures, and because we are weak-willed creatures, the compact we so lately but so sincerely entered into begins to erode. Heady romantic longings are fragile materials with which to construct a relationship. We grow thoughtless and mendacious towards each other. We surprise ourselves with our rudeness. We become deceitful and vindictive.

We may try to persuade the friends who visit us on the weekend to stay a little longer because their regard and their affection remind us of the high expectations the world once had of us. But in our souls, we know we are suffering because there is no one there to nudge us to reform our ways and make an effort. Religions understand this: they know that to sustain goodness, it helps to have an audience. The faiths hence provide us with a gallery of witnesses at the ceremonial beginnings of our marriages and thereafter they entrust a vigilant role to their deities. However sinister the idea of such surveillance may at first seem, it can in truth be reassuring to live as though someone else were continually watching and hoping for the best from us. It is gratifying to feel that our conduct is not simply our own business; it makes the momentous effort of acting nicely seem a little easier.

6.

Libertarians may concede that we would theoretically benefit from guidance, but they still complain that it would be impossible to deliver it, for the simple reason that at heart no one any longer knows what is good and bad. And we don't know, as it is often pointed out in a seductive and dramatic aphorism, because God is dead.

Much of modern moral thought has been transfixed by the idea that a collapse in belief must have irreparably damaged our capacity to build a convincing ethical framework for ourselves. But this argument, while apparently atheistic in nature, owes a strange, unwarranted debt to a religious mindset – for only if we truly believed at some level that God *had* once existed, and that the foundations of morality were therefore in their essence supernatural, would the recognition of his present *non*-existence have any power to shake our moral principles.

However, if we assume from the start that we of course made God up, then the argument rapidly breaks down into a tautology – for why would we bother to feel burdened by ethical doubt if we knew that the many rules ascribed to supernatural beings were actually only the work of our all-too-human ancestors?

It seems clear that the origins of religious ethics lay in the pragmatic need of the earliest communities to control their members' tendencies towards violence, and to foster in them contrary habits of harmony and forgiveness. Religious codes began as cautionary precepts, which were then projected into the sky and reflected back to earth in disembodied and majestic forms. Injunctions to be sympathetic or patient stemmed from an awareness that these were the qualities which could draw societies back from fragmentation and self-destruction. So vital were these rules to our survival that for thousands of years we did not dare to admit that we ourselves had formulated them, lest this expose them to critical scrutiny and irreverent handling. We had to pretend that morality came from the heavens in order to insulate it from our own prevarications and frailties.

But if we can now own up to spiritualizing our ethical laws, we have no cause to do away with the laws themselves. We continue to need exhortations to be sympathetic and just, even if we do not believe that there is a God who has a hand in wishing to make us so. We no longer have to be brought into line by the threat of hell or the promise of paradise; we merely have to be reminded that it is we ourselves – that is, the most mature and reasonable parts of us (seldom present in the midst of our crises and obsessions) – who want to lead the sort of life which we once imagined supernatural beings demanded of us. An adequate evolution of morality from superstition to reason should mean recognizing ourselves as the authors of our own moral commandments.

7.

Of course, our readiness to accept guidance rather depends on the tone in which it is offered. Among religions' more unpalatable features is the tendency of their clergies to speak to people as if they, and they alone, were in possession of maturity and moral authority. And yet Christianity never sounds more beguiling than when it denies this child–adult dichotomy and acknowledges that we are all in the end rather infantile, incomplete, unfinished, easily

We had to invent ways to frighten ourselves into doing what, deep down, we already knew was right: *The Torments of Hell*, French illuminated manuscript, *c.* 1454.

tempted and sinful. We are readier to absorb lessons about virtues and vices if they are delivered by characters who already seem fully acquainted with both categories. Hence the ongoing charm and utility of the idea of Original Sin.

The Judaeo-Christian tradition has intermittently appreciated that what can stop us from reforming ourselves is a lonely, guilty sense of how unusually bad and beyond saving we already are. These religions have therefore proclaimed with considerable sang-froid that all of us, without exception, are appallingly flawed creations. 'Behold, I was brought forth in iniquity; and in sin did my mother conceive me,' thunders the Old Testament (Psalm 51), a message echoed in the New: 'As by one man sin entered into the world, and death by sin; and so death passed upon all men, for that all have sinned' (Romans 5:12).

However, the recognition of this darkness is not the end point which modern pessimism so often assumes it must be. That we are tempted to deceive, steal, insult, egotistically ignore others and be unfaithful is accepted without surprise. The question is not whether we experience shocking temptations but whether we are able once in a while to rise above them.

The doctrine of Original Sin encourages us to inch towards moral improvement by understanding that the faults we despise in ourselves are inevitable features of the species. We can therefore admit to them candidly and attempt to rectify them in the light of day. The doctrine knows that shame is not a helpful emotion for us to be weighed down with as we work towards having a little less to be ashamed about. Enlightenment thinkers believed that they were doing us a favour by declaring man to be originally and naturally good. However, being repeatedly informed of our native decency can cause us to become paralysed with remorse over our failure to measure up to impossible standards of integrity. Confessions of universal sinfulness turn out to be a better starting point from which to take our first modest steps towards virtue.

An emphasis on Original Sin further serves to answer any doubts as to who can have the right to dispense moral advice in a democratic age. To the incensed query, 'And who are you to tell me how to live?', a believer need only push back with the disarming response, 'A fellow sinner'. We are all descended from a single ancestor, the fallen Adam, and are therefore beset by identical anxieties, temptations towards iniquity, cravings for love and occasional aspirations to purity.

8.

We will never discover cast-iron rules of good conduct which will answer every question that might arise about how human beings can live peacefully and well together. However, a lack of absolute agreement on the good life should not in itself be enough to disqualify us from investigating and promoting the theoretical notion of such a life.

The priority of moral instruction must be general, even if the list of virtues and vices to guide any one of us has to be specific, given that we all incline in astonishingly personal ways to idiocy and spite.

The one generalization we might venture to draw from the Judaeo-Christian approach to good behaviour is that we would be advised to focus our attention on relatively small-scale, undramatic kinds of misconduct. Pride, a superficially unobtrusive attitude of mind, was deemed worthy of notice by Christianity, just as Judaism saw nothing frivolous in making recommendations about how often married couples should have sex.

Consider, by contrast, how belatedly and how bluntly the modern state enters into our lives with its injunctions. It intervenes when it is already far too late, after we have picked up the gun, stolen the money, lied to the children or pushed our spouse out of the window. It does not study the debt that large crimes owe to subtle abuses. The achievement of Judaeo-Christian ethics was to encompass more than just the great and obvious vices of mankind. Its recommendations addressed a range of faint cruelties and ill-treatments of the sort which disfigure daily life and form the crucible for cataclysmic crimes. It knew that rudeness and emotional humiliation may be just as corrosive to a well-functioning society as robbery and murder.

The Ten Commandments were a first attempt at reining in man's aggression towards his fellow man. In the edicts of the Talmud and medieval Christian rosters of virtues and vices, we witness an involvement with more modest yet equally treacherous and combustible kinds of mistreatment. It is easy enough to declare that killing and stealing are wrong; it arguably entails a greater feat of the moral imagination to warn against the consequences of making a belittling remark or being sexually aloof.

ii. A Moral Atmosphere

1.

Christianity never minded creating a moral atmosphere in which people could point out their flaws to one another and acknowledge that there was room for improvement in their behaviour.

And, because it saw no particular difference between adults and children, Christianity never balked at offering its followers a range of star-chart equivalents to point them in honourable directions. One of the most accomplished of these is to be found in Padua, under the vaulted brick ceiling of the Scrovegni Chapel.

At the beginning of the fourteenth century, the Florentine artist Giotto was commissioned to decorate the walls of the chapel with a series of frescoes: there were to be fourteen niches, each one containing a portrait allegorizing a different vice or virtue. On the right-hand side of the church, nearest the nave, Giotto painted the so-called cardinal virtues, Prudence, Fortitude, Temperance and Justice, followed by the Christian virtues of Faith, Charity and Hope. Directly opposite these were arrayed a matching configuration of vices: Folly, Inconstancy, Anger, Injustice, Infidelity, Envy and Despair. To each of these abstract titles, the painter appended vivid specimens to evoke viewers' admiration and stir their guilt. Thus Anger is shown tearing apart her garments, screaming at the sky in indignant self-pity, while two niches along, Infidelity squints out with deceitful eyes. The members of the congregation were to sit in their pews and think about which of the virtues they had embraced and which of the vices they had fallen prey to, while God watched over them from the celestial sphere, stars in hand.

Anger   Inconstancy   Envy

Temperance   Fortitude   Charity

Giotto, *The Vices and the Virtues*, Scrovegni Chapel, Padua, *c.* 1304.

The religious tradition to which Giotto's star chart belonged felt comfortable in making detailed proposals about how one should behave and in distinguishing what it plainly termed good from its opposite. Depictions of vices and virtues were ubiquitous – in the backs of Bibles, in prayer books, on the walls of churches and public buildings – and their purpose was straightforwardly didactic: they were meant to provide a compass by which the faithful could steer their lives in honourable directions.

2.

By contrast with this Christian desire to generate a moral atmosphere, libertarian theorists have argued that public space should be kept neutral. There should be no reminders of kindness on the walls of our buildings or in the pages of our books. Such messages would, after all, constitute dramatic infringements on our much-prized 'liberty'.

However, we have already seen why this concern for liberty doesn't necessarily honour our deepest wishes, given our compulsive and wayward natures. We can also now admit that, in any case, our public spaces are not even remotely neutral. They are – as a quick glance down any high street will reveal – covered with commercial messages. Even in societies theoretically dedicated to leaving us free to make our own choices, our minds are continuously manipulated in directions we hardly consciously recognize. It is sometimes said by advertising agencies, in a prophylactic attempt at false modesty, that advertising does not really *work*. We are adults, this argument holds, and so do not lose our capacity for reason the instant we set eyes on a beautifully photographed

billboard or catalogue. It is granted that children may be less reso-
lute and could therefore need shielding from certain messages on
television before eight o'clock in the evening, lest they conceive
a maniacal craving for a particular train set or carbonated drink.
But adults are apparently sensible and self-controlled enough not
to alter their values or consumption patterns simply on account of
an unceasing array of artfully created messages which reach them
from every side and medium at all times of day and night.

However, this distinction between child and adult is suspi-
ciously convenient to commercial interests. In truth, we are all
fragile in our commitments and suffer from a weakness of will
in relation to the siren calls of advertising, an ill-tempered three-
year-old entranced by the sight of a farmyard play set with inflat-
able dog kennel as much as a forty-two-year-old captivated by the
possibilities of a barbecue set with added tongs and hotplate.

3.

Atheists tend to pity the inhabitants of religiously dominated societies for the extent of the propaganda they have to endure, but this
is to overlook secular societies' equally powerful and continuous
calls to prayer. A libertarian state truly worthy of the name would
try to redress the balance of messages that reach its citizens away
from the merely commercial and towards a holistic conception of
flourishing. True to the ambitions of Giotto's frescoes, these new
messages would render vivid to us the many noble ways of behaving that we currently admire so much and so blithely ignore.

We simply will not care for very long about the higher values
when all we are given to convince us of their worth is an occasional

We don't only need reminders of the advantages of savoury snacks.

reminder in a modestly selling, largely ignored book of essays by a so-called philosopher – while, in the city beyond, the superlative talents of the globe's advertising agencies perform their phantas-magorical alchemy and set our every sensory fibre alight in the name of a new kind of cleaning product or savoury snack.

If we tend to think so often about lemon-scented floor polish or cracked black pepper crisps, but relatively little about endurance or justice, the fault is not merely our own. It is also that these two cardinal virtues are not generally in a position to become clients of Young & Rubicam.

iii. Role Models

1.

While paying attention to the messages in its public spaces, Christianity also wisely recognizes the extent to which our concepts of good and bad are shaped by the people we spend time with. It knows that we are dangerously permeable with regard to our social circle, all too apt to internalize and mimic others' attitudes and behaviour. Simultaneously, it accepts that the particular company we keep is largely a result of haphazard forces, a peculiar cast of characters drawn from our childhood, schooling, community and work. Among the few hundred people we regularly encounter, not very many are likely to be the sorts of exceptional individuals who exhaust our imagination with their good qualities, who strengthen our soul and whose voices we want consciously to adopt to bolster our best impulses.

2.

The paucity of paragons helps to explain why Catholicism sets before its believers some two and a half thousand of the greatest, most virtuous human beings who, it feels, have ever lived. These saints are each in their different ways exemplars of qualities we should hope to nurture in ourselves. St Joseph, for instance, may teach us how to cope calmly with the pressures of a young family and how to face the trials of the workplace with a modest and uncomplaining temper. There are moments when we may want to break down and sob in the company of St Jude, patron saint of lost causes, whose gentle manner can grant us comfort without

An opportunity to remember friends: the months of November and December, from a sixteenth-century English psalter, tabling the deathdays of, among others, Sts Hugh, Katherine, Theodore, Edmund, Clement, Barbara, Lucy and Osmund.

any need to find immediate solutions or even hope. At times of anxiety, we could turn to St Philip Neri, who would never under-play our problems or humiliate us but would know how to tease out our sense of the absurd and make us laugh therapeutically at our condition. We might find it particularly consoling to guess at how the imperturbable St Philip would handle the hazards of a family reunion or the crash of a computer's hard drive.

To further enhance our imaginative connections with the saints, Catholicism provides us with calendars that list their deathdays, so that we may have regular occasion to withdraw from our social circle and contemplate the lives of people who gave away all their money and wandered the earth doing good works while wearing a rough tunic to mortify the flesh (St Francis) or who used their faith in God to magically reattach a severed ear to its distressed owner's head (St Cuthbert).

3.

In addition, Catholicism perceives that there is a benefit to being able to see our ideal friends around the house in miniaturized three-dimensional representations. After all, most of us began our lives by having nurturing relationships with bears and other animals, to whom we would talk and be tacitly addressed by in turn. Though immobile, these animals were nevertheless skilful at conveying their consoling and inspiring personalities to us. We would talk to them when we were sad and were comforted when we looked across the bedroom and saw them stoically enduring the night on our behalf. Catholicism sees no reason to abandon the mechanics of such relationships and so invites us to buy wood,

What would he do next? St Francis of Assisi for sale in a variety of formats.

stone, resin or plastic versions of the saints and place them on shelves or alcoves in our rooms and hallways. At times of domestic chaos, we can look across at a plastic statuette and inwardly ask what St Francis of Assisi would recommend that we say to our furious wife and hysterical children now. The answer may be inside us all along, but it doesn't usually emerge or become effective until we go through the exercise of formally asking the question of a saintly figurine.

4.

A well-functioning secular society would think with similar care about its role models. It would not only provide us with film stars and singers. An absence of religious belief in no way invalidates a continuing need for 'patron saints' of qualities like Courage, Friendship, Fidelity, Patience, Confidence or Scepticism. We can still profit from moments when we give internal space to the voices of people who are more balanced, brave and generous-spirited than we are – Lincoln or Whitman, Churchill or Stendhal, Warren Buffett or Paul Smith – and through whom we may reconnect with our most dignified and serious possibilities.

5.

The religious perspective on morality suggests that it is in the end a sign of immaturity to object too strenuously to being treated like a child. The libertarian obsession with freedom ignores how much of our original childhood need for constraint and guidance endures within us, and therefore how much we stand to learn from paternalistic strategies. It is not very kind, nor ultimately

even very freeing, to be deemed so grown up that one is left alone
to do entirely as one pleases.

Even the greatest atheists may benefit from role models. *Above*: Sigmund Freud's desk in London, covered in the statuettes of Assyrian, Egyptian, Chinese and Roman figurines. *Top*: Or one might prefer Virginia Woolf.

IV

Education

'The object of universities is not to make skilful lawyers, physicians or engineers. It is to make capable and cultivated *human beings*,' John Stuart Mill.

i. What We Get Taught

1.

A busy high street in north London. In a neighbourhood studded with Cypriot bakeries, Jamaican hairdressers and Bengali takeaways, stands the campus of one of Britain's newest universities. It is dominated by a twelve-storey asymmetrical steel tower which houses, along a series of corridors painted a vivid purple and yellow, the lecture theatres and seminar rooms of the Department of the Humanities.

Across the university, 200,000 undergraduates are enrolled on 400 different degree programmes. This particular department was inaugurated just a few months ago by a minister for education and a cousin of the Queen, in a ceremony now commemorated on an engraved granite block embedded in a wall near the toilets.

'A home for "*The best that has been said and thought in the world*"', reads the plaque, borrowing Matthew Arnold's famous definition of culture. The quote must have struck a chord with the university, for it reappears in the undergraduate admissions handbook and in a mural by the drinks dispenser in the basement cafeteria.

There are few things that secular society believes in as fervently as education. Since the Enlightenment, education – from primary level through to university – has been presented as the most effective answer to a range of society's gravest ills; the conduit to fashioning a civilized, prosperous and rational citizenry.

A look at the degree courses offered by the new university reveals that over half are intended to equip undergraduates with practical skills, the sort required for successful careers in mercantile, technological societies: courses in chemistry, business, microbiology, law, marketing and public health.

But the grander claims made on behalf of education, the sort one reads of in prospectuses or hears about in graduation ceremonies, tend to imply that colleges and universities are more than mere factories for turning out technocrats and industrialists. The suggestion is that they have a yet higher task to fulfil: they may turn us into better, wiser and happier people.

As John Stuart Mill, another Victorian defender of the aims of education, put it: 'The object of universities is not to make skilful lawyers, physicians or engineers. It is to make capable and cultivated *human beings*.' Or, to go back to Matthew Arnold, a proper cultural education should inspire in us 'a love of our neighbour, a desire for clearing human confusion and for diminishing human misery'. At its most ambitious, he added, it should engender nothing less than the 'noble aspiration to leave the world better and happier than we found it'.

2.

What unites such ambitious and beguiling claims is their passion – and their vagueness. It is seldom clear how education could turn students towards generosity and truth and away from sin and error, though it is typically hard to do anything other than passively lend one's assent to this inspiring notion, given its familiarity and its sheer beauty.

Nevertheless, it would be no injustice to examine the high-flown rhetoric in the light of certain realities on the ground, as revealed by an ordinary Monday afternoon in the Faculty of the Humanities in the modern university in north London.

The choice of department is not coincidental, for the transformative and lyrical claims made on behalf of education have almost always been connected to the humanities rather than endocrinology or biostatistics. It is the study of philosophy, history, art, the classics, languages and literature that has been thought to yield the most complex, subtle and therapeutic dimensions of the educational experience.

In a corner classroom on the seventh floor, a group of second-year history students are following a lecture about agricultural reform in eighteenth-century France. The argument made by their professor, who has spent twenty years researching the subject, is that the cause of declining crop yields between 1742 and 1798 had less to do with bad harvests than with the relatively low price of agricultural land, which encouraged landlords to invest their money in trade rather than farming.

On the floor below, in the classics department, fifteen students are comparing the use of natural imagery in the works of the Roman poets Horace and Petronius. The professor is pointing out that while Horace identifies nature with lawlessness and decay, Petronius, in many ways the more pessimistic of the two poets, reveres it for precisely the opposite qualities. Perhaps because the air ventilation system has broken down and the windows have jammed shut, the atmosphere is a little sluggish. Few students seem to be following the argument

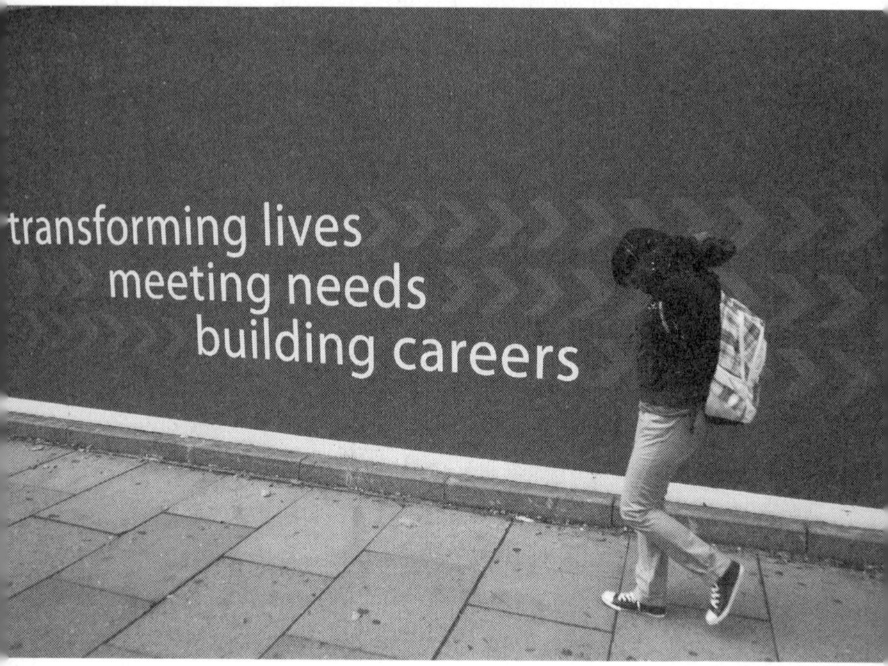
transforming lives
meeting needs
building careers

with the intent the professor might have hoped for when he was awarded his PhD in Oxford twenty years ago ('Patterns of Meta-narrative in Euripides' *Ion*').

The application of the university's academics to their tasks is intense and moving. And yet it is hard to see how the content of their courses and the direction of their examination questions bear any significant relationship to Arnold's and Mill's ideals. Whatever rhetoric may be rehearsed in its prospectuses, the modern university appears to have precious little interest in teaching its students any emotional or ethical life skills, much less how to love their neighbours and leave the world happier than they found it.

The prerequisites for a BA in philosophy, for example, are limited to a familiarity with the central topics of metaphysics (substance, individuation, universals) and the completion of a thesis on concepts of intentionality in Quine, Frege or Putnam. An equivalent degree in English literature will be awarded to those who can successfully tackle *The Waste Land* on allegorical and anagogic levels and trace the influence of Seneca's dramatic theories on the development of Jacobean theatre.

Graduation speeches stereotypically identify liberal education with the acquisition of wisdom and self-knowledge, but these goals have little bearing on the day-to-day methods of departmental instruction and examination. To judge by what they do rather than what they airily declaim, universities are in the business of turning out a majority of tightly focused professionals (lawyers, physicians, engineers) and a minority of culturally well-informed but ethically confused arts graduates aptly panicked about how they might remuneratively occupy the rest of their lives.

We have implicitly charged our higher-education system with a dual and possibly contradictory mission: to teach us how to make a living and to teach us how to live. And we have left the second of these two aims recklessly vague and unattended.

3.

Who cares? Why should we be worrying about the shortcomings of university education in a book ostensibly concerned with religion?

The reasons start to become clear when we consider the relationship between the decline in the teaching of scripture and the rise in the teaching of culture. When religious belief began to fracture in Europe in the early nineteenth century, anguished questions were raised about how, in the absence of a Christian framework, people would manage to find meaning, understand themselves, behave in a moral fashion, forgive their fellow humans and confront their own mortality. And in answer, it was proposed by an influential faction that cultural works might henceforth be consulted in place of the biblical texts. Culture could replace scripture.

The hope was that culture might be no less effective than religion (which was understood to mean Christianity) in its ability to guide, humanize and console. Histories, paintings, philosophical ideas and fictional narratives could all be mined to yield lessons not far removed in their ethical tenor and emotional impact from those taught by the Bible. One would be able to have meaning unburdened by superstition. The maxims of Marcus Aurelius, the poetry of Boccaccio, the operas of

How to live was not on the curriculum. Graduation ceremony, Oxford University.

Wagner and the paintings of Turner could be secular society's new sacraments.

On the basis of such notions, whole subject areas which had never before been included in formal education began to enter the curricula of universities in Europe and the United States. Literature, previously dismissed as being worthy of study only by adolescent girls and convalescents, was recognized as a serious subject fit for analysis within Western universities during the second half of the nineteenth century. The newfound prestige of novels and poems was based on the realization that these forms, much like the Gospels, could deliver complex moral messages embedded within emotionally charged narratives, and thereby prompt affective identification and self-examination. In his inaugural lecture at Oxford University in 1922, George Gordon, Merton Professor of Literature, emphasized the scale of the task that had fallen to his field: 'England is sick, and ... English literature must save it. The Churches (as I understand) having failed, and social remedies being slow, English literature now has a triple function: still, I suppose, to delight and instruct us, but also, and above all, to save our souls and heal the State.'

4.
Claims that culture could stand in for scripture – that *Middlemarch* could take up the responsibilities previously handled by the Psalms, or the essays of Schopenhauer satisfy needs once catered for by St Augustine's *City of God* – still have a way of sounding eccentric or insane in their combination of impiety and ambition.

Nevertheless, perhaps the proposition is not so much absurd as it is unfamiliar. The very qualities that the religious locate in their holy texts can often just as well be discovered in works of culture. Novels and historical narratives can adeptly impart moral instruction and edification. Great paintings do make suggestions about our requirements for happiness. Philosophy can usefully address our anxieties and offer consolations. Literature can change our lives. Equivalents to the ethical lessons of religion do lie scattered across the cultural canon.

Why, then, does the notion of replacing religion with culture, of living according to the lessons of literature and art as believers will according to the lessons of faith, continue to sound so peculiar to us? Why are atheists not able to draw on culture with the same spontaneity and rigour which the religious apply to their holy texts?

This acknowledgement of our inhibitions brings us back to the influence of that foremost upholder and propagator of culture in the modern world, the university. The methodologies which universities today employ in disseminating culture are fundamentally at odds with the intense, neo-religious ambitions once harboured by lapsed or sceptical Christians such as Arnold and Mill. While universities have achieved unparalleled expertise in imparting factual information about culture, they remain wholly uninterested in training students to use it as a repertoire of wisdom – this latter term referring to a kind of knowledge concerned with things which are not only true but also inwardly beneficial, a knowledge which can prove of solace to us when confronted by the infinite

A student of medieval literature, Oxford University.

challenges of existence, from a tyrannical employer to a fatal lesion on our liver.

We are by no means lacking in material which we might call into service to replace the holy texts; we are simply treating that material in the wrong way. We are unwilling to consider secular culture *religiously* enough, in other words, as a source of guidance. So opposed have many atheists been to the content of religious belief that they have omitted to appreciate its inspiring and still valid overall object: to provide us with well-structured advice on how to lead our lives.

5.

The differences between secular and religious approaches to education boil down to the question of what learning should be for.

It is a question which tends to vex those in charge of teaching culture in secular institutions. Enquiries as to why, exactly, people should bother to study history or literature usually strike them as impertinent and argumentative and are often left unanswered. Academics in the humanities appreciate that their opposite numbers in the technical and scientific departments can without trouble justify their work in utilitarian terms to impatient government officials and donors (in the unlikely event that anyone should idly wonder what the purpose of rocket science or public health might be). But fearing that they cannot compete effectively against these rivals, the denizens of the humanities prefer to take refuge in ambiguity and silence, having carefully calculated that they retain just enough prestige to get away with leaving the reasons for their existence somewhat murky.

When confronted by those who demand of culture that it should be relevant and useful, that it should offer up advice on how to choose a career or survive the end of a marriage, how to contain sexual impulses or cope with the news of a medical death sentence, the guardians of culture become disdainful. Their ideal audiences are students who are uninclined to drama and self-involvement, who are mature, independent, temperamentally able to live with questions rather than answers and ready to put aside their own needs for the sake of years of disinterested study of agricultural yields in eighteenth-century Normandy or the presence of the infinite in Kant's noumenal realm.

6.

Christianity meanwhile looks at the purpose of education from another angle, because it has an entirely different concept of human nature. It has no patience with theories that dwell on our independence or our maturity. It instead believes us to be at heart desperate, fragile, vulnerable, sinful creatures, a good deal less wise than we are knowledgeable, always on the verge of anxiety, tortured by our relationships, terrified of death – and most of all in need of God.

What sort of education might benefit such forlorn wretches? While the capacity for abstract thought is considered by Christianity to be in no way dishonourable, and indeed even a potential sign of divine grace, it is held to be of secondary importance to a more practical ability to bring consoling and nurturing ideas to bear on our disturbed and irresolute selves.

We are familiar enough with the major categories of the humanities as they are taught in secular universities – history and anthropology, literature and philosophy – as well as with the sorts of examination questions they produce: Who were the Carolingians? Where did phenomenology originate? What did Emerson want? We know too that this scheme leaves the emotional aspects of our characters to develop spontaneously, or at the very least in private, perhaps when we are with our families or out on solitary walks in the countryside.

In contrast, Christianity concerns itself from the outset with the inner confused side of us, declaring that we are none of us born knowing how to live; we are by nature fragile and capricious, unempathetic and beset by fantasies of omnipotence, worlds away from being able to command even a modicum of the good sense and calm that secular education takes as the starting point for its own pedagogy.

Christianity is focused on helping a part of us that secular language struggles even to name, which is not precisely intelligence or emotion, not character or personality, but another, even more abstract entity loosely connected with all of those and yet differentiated from them by an additional ethical and transcendent dimension – and to which we may as well refer, following Christian terminology, as the *soul*. It has been the essential task of the Christian pedagogic machine to nurture, reassure, comfort and guide our souls.

Throughout its history, Christianity indulged in lengthy debates as to the nature of the soul, speculating on what it might look like, where it might be located and how it might

The baby inside us that we must educate. Receiving one's soul: illumination from
an early fifteenth-century Bible.

best be educated. In its origins, the soul was thought by theologians to resemble a miniature baby inserted by God into an infant's mouth at the moment of his or her birth.

At the other end of the individual's life, at the moment of death, the soul-baby would then be expelled again through his or her mouth. The trajectory it was to follow would be more ambiguous this time: it would be either taken up by God or snatched away by the Devil, depending on how well or badly its owner had tended to it over the years. A good soul was one that had managed to find appropriate answers to the great questions and tensions of existence, a soul marked by such godly virtues as faith, hope, charity and love.

Differ though we might with Christianity's view of what precisely our souls need, it is hard to discredit the provocative underlying thesis, which seems no less relevant in the secular realm than in the religious one – that we have within us a precious, childlike, vulnerable core which we should nourish and nurture on its turbulent journey through life.

By its own standards, Christianity therefore has no choice but to tilt its educational emphasis towards explicit questions: How can we manage to live together? How do we tolerate others' faults? How can we accept our own limitations and assuage our anger? A degree of urgent didacticism is a requirement rather than an insult. The difference between Christian and secular education reveals itself with particular clarity in their respective characteristic modes of instruction: secular education delivers *lectures*, Christianity *sermons*. Expressed in terms of intent, we might say that one is concerned with imparting information,

An illumination from an early-fifteenth-century Book of Hours, showing a soul which has recently emerged from a deceased man and is being fought over by the Devil and St Michael.

the other with changing our lives. Sermons by their very nature assume that their audiences are in important ways lost. The titles alone of the sermons by one of the most famous preachers of eighteenth-century England, John Wesley, show Christianity seeking to dispense practical advice about a range of the soul's ordinary challenges: 'On Being Kind', 'On Staying Obedient to Parents', 'On Visiting the Sick', 'On Caution Against Bigotry'. Unlikely though it seems that Wesley's sermons could ever seduce atheists through their content, they nevertheless succeed, like any number of Christian texts, in categorizing knowledge under useful headings.

While it was at first hoped by Arnold, Mill and others that universities could deliver secular sermons that would tell us how to avoid bigotry and find helpful things to say when visiting ill people, these centres of learning have never offered the kind of guidance that churches have focused on, from a belief that academia should refrain from making any associations between cultural works and individual sorrows. It would be a shocking affront to university etiquette to ask what *Tess of the d'Urbervilles* might usefully teach us about love, or to suggest that the novels of Henry James might be read with an eye to discovering parables about staying honest in a slippery mercantile world.

Yet a search for parables is precisely what lies at the heart of the Christian approach to texts. Wesley himself was a profoundly scholarly man in ways that the modern university would honour. He had an intimate textual knowledge of Leviticus and Matthew, Corinthians and Luke, but he quoted verses

Teaching wisdom rather than knowledge: John Wesley, a sermon outdoors in York, 1746.

from these only when they could be integrated into a parabolic structure and used to leaven the hardships of his listeners. Like all Christian sermonizers, he looked to culture principally as a tool, asking of any biblical passage what general rules of conduct it could exemplify and promote.

In the secular sphere, we may well be reading the right books, but we too often fail to ask direct questions of them, declining to advance sufficiently vulgar, neo-religious enquiries because we are embarrassed to admit to the true nature of our inner needs. We are fatefully in love with ambiguity, uncritical of the Modernist doctrine that great art should have no moral content or desire to change its audience. Our resistance to a parabolic methodology stems from a confused distaste for utility, didacticism and simplicity, and from an unquestioned assumption that anything a child could understand must of necessity be infantile in nature.

Yet Christianity holds that, despite outward appearances, important parts of us retain the elemental structures of earliest childhood. Just like children, therefore, we need assistance. Knowledge must be fed to us slowly and carefully, like food cut into manageable bites. Any more than a few lessons in a day will exhaust us unduly. Twelve lines of Deuteronomy may be enough, for instance, along with a few explanatory notes which point out in plain language what there is for us to notice and to feel therein.

The techniques that the academy so fears – the emphasis on the connection between abstract ideas and our own lives, the lucid interpretation of texts, the preference for extracts over wholes – have always been the methods of religions, which had to wrestle, centuries before the invention of television, with the challenge of how to render ideas vivid and pertinent to impatient and distracted audiences. They have realized all along that the greatest danger they faced was not the oversimplification of concepts but the erosion of interest and support through incomprehension and apathy. They recognized that clarity preserves rather than undermines ideas, for it creates a base upon which the intellectual labour of an elite can subsequently rest. Christianity was confident that its precepts were robust enough to be understood at a variety of levels, that they could be presented in the form of crude woodcuts to the yeomen of the parish church or discussed in Latin by theologians at the University of Bologna, and that each iteration would endorse and reinforce the others.

In the preface to a volume of his collected sermons, John Wesley explained and defended his adherence to simplicity: 'I design plain truth for plain people: therefore ... I abstain from all nice and philosophical speculations; from all perplexed and intricate reasonings; and, as far as possible, from even the show of learning. My design is ... to forget all that ever I have read in my life.'

A handful of brave secular writers have been able to express themselves with a similarly inspiring openness, among the most notable being Donald Winnicott in the field of psychoanalysis and Ralph Waldo Emerson in literature. But these characters have been regrettably few in number, and most have also drawn upon a religious background to mould and buttress their sensibilities (Winnicott began as a Methodist, Emerson as a Transcendentalist).

The greatest Christian preachers have been *vulgar* in the very best sense. While not surrendering any of their claims to complexity or insight, they have wished to help those who came to hear them.

7.

By contrast, we have constructed an intellectual world whose most celebrated institutions rarely consent to ask, let alone answer, the most serious questions of the soul. To address the incoherencies of the situation, we might begin to overhaul our universities by doing away with fields like history and literature, ultimately superficial categories which, even if they cover valuable material, do not in themselves track the themes that most torment and attract our souls.

The redesigned universities of the future would draw upon the same rich catalogue of culture treated by their traditional counterparts, likewise promoting the study of novels, histories, plays and paintings, but they would teach this material with a view to illuminating students' lives rather than merely prodding at academic goals. *Anna Karenina* and *Madame Bovary* would thus be assigned in a course on understanding the tensions of marriage instead of in one focused on narrative trends in nineteenth-century fiction, just as the recommendations of Epicurus and Seneca would appear in the syllabus for a course about dying rather than in a survey of Hellenistic philosophy.

Departments would be required to confront the problematic areas of our lives head-on. Notions of assistance and transformation which presently hover ghost-like over speeches at graduation ceremonies would be given form and explored as openly in lay institutions as they are in churches. There would be classes in, among other topics, being alone, reconsidering work, improving relationships with children, reconnecting with nature and facing illness. A university alive to the true responsibilities of cultural artefacts within a secular age would establish a Department for Relationships, an Institute of Dying and a Centre for Self-Knowledge.

In this way, as Arnold and Mill would have wished, secular education would start to outgrow the fears it associates with relevance and redesign its curricula to engage directly with our most pressing personal and ethical dilemmas.

Few would fall asleep.

ii. How We Are Taught

1.

Rearranging university education according to the insights gained from religion would entail adjusting not only the curriculum but also, just as crucially, the way it is taught.

In its methods, Christianity has from its beginnings been guided by a simple yet essential observation that has nevertheless never made any impression upon those in charge of secular education: how very easily we forget things.

Its theologians have known that our soul suffers from what ancient Greek philosophers termed *akrasia*, a perplexing tendency to know what we should do combined with a persistent reluctance actually to do it, whether through weakness of will or absent-mindedness. We all possess wisdom that we lack the strength properly to enact in our lives. Christianity pictures the mind as a sluggish and fickle organ, easy enough to impress but forever inclined to change its focus and cast its commitments aside. Consequently, the religion proposes that the central issue for education is not so much how to counteract ignorance – as secular educators imply – as how we can combat our reluctance to act upon ideas which we have already fully understood at a theoretical level. It follows the Greek sophists in insisting that all lessons should appeal to both reason (*logos*) and emotion (*pathos*), as well as endorsing Cicero's advice that public speakers should have a threefold ability to prove (*probare*), delight (*delectare*) and persuade (*flectere*). There is no justification for delivering world-shaking ideas in a mumble.

2.

However, defenders of secular university education have seldom worried about *akrasia*. They implicitly maintain that people will be properly affected by concepts even when they hear about them only once or twice, at the age of twenty, before a fifty-year career in finance or market research, via a lecturer standing in a bare room speaking in a monotone. According to this view, ideas may fall out of the mind in much the same random order as the contents of an upturned handbag, or may be expressed with all the graceless banality of an instruction manual, without threatening the overall purpose of intellectual endeavour. Ever since Plato attacked the Greek sophists for being more concerned with speaking well than thinking honestly, Western intellectuals have been intransigently suspicious of eloquence, whether spoken or written, believing that the fluent pedagogue could unfairly disguise unacceptable or barren notions with honeyed words. The way an idea is imparted has been deemed to be of little importance next to the quality of the idea itself. The modern university has thus placed no premium on a talent for oratory, priding itself on its interest in the truth rather than in techniques to ensure its successful and enduring conveyance.

It seems beyond imagining that any contemporary university lecturer would, upon his death, have his body strapped to a table, his neck cut open and his larynx, tongue and lower jaw removed, to be mounted in a golden case encrusted with jewels and displayed in a niche at the centre of a shrine dedicated to the memory of his oratorical gifts. Yet this was precisely the fate

This rarely happens to our university lecturers: the enshrined lower jaw of
St Anthony of Padua, reliquary, basilica of St Anthony, Padua, *c.* 1350.

of Anthony of Padua, the thirteenth-century Franciscan friar who acceded to sainthood by virtue of his exceptional talent and stamina for public speaking, and whose vocal apparatus, on view in the basilica of his hometown, still draws admiring pilgrims from all corners of Christendom. According to holy legend, Anthony delivered 10,000 sermons over his lifetime and was able to melt the hearts of the most determined sinners. It was even said that one day in Rimini, standing on the sea-shore, he began to declaim to no one in particular and soon found himself surrounded by an audience of curious and evidently appreciative fish.

3.

St Anthony was but one exemplar in a long and self-conscious tradition of Christian oratory. The preaching of John Donne, the Jacobean poet and dean of St Paul's Cathedral, was comparably persuasive, treating complex ideas with an impression of effortless lucidity. Forestalling the possibility of boredom during his sermons, Donne would pause every few paragraphs to sum up his thoughts in phrases designed to engrave themselves on his listeners' skittish minds ('Age is a sicknesse, and youth is an ambush'). Like all compelling aphorists, he had a keen command of binary oppositions ('If you take away due fear, you take away true love'), in his case married to a lyrical sensibility which enabled him to soar along contrails of rare adjectives before bringing his congregation up short with a maxim of homespun simplicity ('Never send to know for whom the bell tolls; it tolls for thee'). He situated himself vis-à-vis his

St Anthony preaching to carp, sixteenth-century illuminated manuscript.

audience without any hint of schoolmasterly pedantry. They could feel the truth of his ideas all the more intensely for it being delivered by someone who appeared to be appealingly human and flawed ('I throw myself down in my chamber, and I call in, and invite God, and his Angels thither, and when they are there, I neglect God and his Angels, for the noise of a fly, for the rattling of a coach, for the whining of a door').

More recently, the Christian oratorical tradition has been further developed by African-American preachers, particularly those of the Pentecostal and Baptist denominations. In churches across the United States, a Sunday sermon is not an occasion to sit with one eye trained on the clock while, from a lectern in the apse, a cleric impassively dissects the story of the Good Samaritan. Instead, believers are expected to open their hearts, clasp the hands of their neighbours, erupt into shouts of 'All right now' and 'Amen, preacher', let the Holy Spirit enter their souls and finally collapse in paroxysms of ecstatic wailing. Up on the stage, the preacher stokes the fires of his congregation's enthusiasm through call-and-response, asking repeatedly, in a mesmerizing blend of vernacular expression and the vocabulary of the King James Bible, 'Will you say Amen? I say will you *say* Amen?'

However powerful any proposition may be, it becomes so much more so in front of a crowd of 500 people who exclaim in unison after every point:

'... Thank you, Jesus.'

'... Thank you, Saviour.'

'... Thank you, Christ.'

'... Thank you, Lord.'

Could a lecture on Walt Whitman be as moving?

There is little chance of resisting a theological argument which flows like this one, from the stage of the New Vision Baptist Church in Knoxville, Tennessee:

'None of us today is in jail.'

(*'Amen, All right now, Amen, Preacher,'* say the members of the congregation)

'Lord have mercy.'

(*'Amen.'*)

'So, brothers, sisters, we should never be in prison in our minds.'

(*'Amen, Preacher.'*)

'Do you hear me, my brothers and sisters?'

(*'Amen, amen, amen!'*)

The contrast with the typical lecture in the humanities could hardly be more damning. And unnecessary. What purpose can possibly be served by the academy's primness? How much more expansive the scope of meaning in Montaigne's essays would seem if a 100-strong and transported chorus were to voice its approval after every sentence. How much longer might Rousseau's philosophical truths linger in our consciousness if they were structured around rhythmical verses of call-and-response. Secular education will never succeed in reaching its potential until humanities lecturers are sent to be trained by African-American Pentecostal preachers. Only then will our timid pedagogues be able to shake off their inhibitions during lectures on Keats or Adam Smith and, unconstrained by false notions of propriety, call out to their comatose audiences, 'Do you hear me? I say do you *hear* me?' And only *then* will their now-tearful students fall to their knees, ready to let the spirit of some of the world's most important ideas enter and transform them.

4.

Aside from needing to be delivered eloquently, ideas also have to be repeated to us constantly. Three or five or ten times a day, we must be forcibly reminded of truths that we love but otherwise will not be able to hold on to. What we read at nine in the morning we will have forgotten by lunchtime and will need to reread by dusk. Our inner lives must be lent a structure and our best thoughts reinforced to counter the continuous pull of distraction and disintegration.

Religions have been wise enough to establish elaborate calendars and schedules which lay claim to the lengths as well as the depths of their followers' lives, letting no month, day or hour escape without administration of a precisely calibrated dose of ideas. In the detailed way in which they tell the faithful what to read, think, sing and do at almost every moment, religious agendas seem at once sublimely obsessive and calmingly thorough. The Book of Common Prayer, for instance, decrees that its subscribers should always gather at six-thirty in the evening on the twenty-sixth Sunday after Trinity, as the candlelight throws shadows against the chapel walls, to listen to a reading from the second section of the deuterocanonical Book of Baruch, just as on 25 January they must always think of the Conversion of St Paul, and on the morning of 2 July reflect on the Visitation of the Blessed Virgin Mary and imbibe the moral lessons of Job 3. Schedules are more exacting still for Catholics, whose days are punctuated by no fewer than seven occasions for prayer. Every evening at ten they must, for example, scan their consciences, read a Psalm, declare *In manus tuas, Domine* ('Into your hands, Lord'), sing the *Nunc dimittis* from the second chapter of the Gospel of St Luke and conclude with a hymn to the mother of Jesus ('Virgin now and always, take pity on us sinners').

How free secular society leaves us by contrast. It expects that we will spontaneously find our way to the ideas that matter to us and gives us weekends off for consumption and recreation. Like science, it privileges discovery. It associates repetition with punitive shortage, presenting us with an incessant stream of new information – and therefore it prompts us to forget everything.

For example, we are enticed to go to the cinema to see a newly released film, which ends up moving us to an exquisite pitch of sensitivity, sorrow and excitement. We leave the theatre vowing to reconsider our entire existence in light of the values shown on screen, and to purge ourselves of our decadence and haste. And yet by the following evening, after a day of meetings and aggravations, our cinematic experience is well on its way towards obliteration, just like so much else which once impressed us but which we soon enough came to discard: the majesty of the ruins of Ephesus, the view from Mount Sinai, the poetry recital in Edinburgh, the feelings we had after putting down Tolstoy's *The Death of Ivan Ilyich*. In the end, all modern artists share something of the bathetic condition

16

Table III
ORDER FOR GOSPEL READING
FOR SUNDAYS IN ORDINARY TIME

Luke's Gospel represents Jesus' journey from Galilee to
Jerusalem – a journey which is completed in the Acts of the
Apostles by the journey of the Church from Jerusalem to the
ends of the earth. The Lectionary in the year of Luke represents
faithfully his 'Travel Narrative' (chapters 9-19) – Jesus' journey to
death, to resurrection and his return to the Father (see

Unit I	The figure of Jesus the Messiah	Sundays 1-2
SUNDAY 1	The baptism of Jesus	Lk 3:15-16, 21-22
SUNDAY 2	The marriage feast at Cana	Jn 2:1-12
Unit II	Luke's programme for Jesus' ministry	Sundays 3-4
SUNDAY 3	Prologue. The visit to Nazareth (1)	Lk 1:1-4; 4:14-21
SUNDAY 4	The visit to Nazareth (2)	Lk 4:21-30
Unit III	The Galilean Ministry	Sundays 5-12
SUNDAY 5	'The call of the first apostles	Lk 5:1-11
SUNDAY 6	The sermon on the plain (1)	Lk 6:17, 20-26
SUNDAY 7	The sermon on the plain (2)	Lk 6:27-38
SUNDAY 8	The sermon on the plain (3)	Lk 6:39-45
SUNDAY 9	The cure of the centurion's servant	Lk 7:1-10
SUNDAY 10	'The Widow of Nain	Lk 7:11-17
SUNDAY 11	'Jesus' feet anointed, the sinful woman	Lk 7:36-8:3
SUNDAY 12	Peter's confession of faith	Lk 9:18-24
Unit IV	The first part of the 'Travel Narrative'. The qualities Jesus demands of those who follow him	Sundays 13-23
SUNDAY 13	'The journey to Jerusalem begins	Lk 9:51-62
SUNDAY 14	'The mission of the seventy-two	Lk 10:1-12, 17-20
SUNDAY 15	'The Good Samaritan	Lk 10:25-37
SUNDAY 16	'Martha and Mary	Lk 10:38-42
SUNDAY 17	'The importunate friend	Lk 11:1-13
SUNDAY 18	'The parable of the rich fool	Lk 12:13-21
SUNDAY 19	The need for vigilance	Lk 12:32-48
SUNDAY 20	'Not peace but division'	Lk 12:49-53
SUNDAY 21	Few will be saved	Lk 13:22-30
SUNDAY 22	True humility	Lk 14:1, 7-14
SUNDAY 23	The cost of discipleship	Lk 14:25-33

17

YEAR C: YEAR OF LUKE

Sundays 13-31). Luke's vision of the journey is not geographical
or chronological. Rather it is seen as a journey for the whole
Church and for the individual christian, a journey towards
suffering and glory. Each Gospel passage should mean a great
deal more to preacher and reader when it is seen in the context of
the whole programme of readings for Year C.

Unit V	The 'Gospel within the Gospel': the message of pardon and reconciliation – the parables of God's mercy	Sunday 24
SUNDAY 24	'The lost coin, the lost sheep, and the prodigal son	Lk 15:1-32
Unit VI	The second part of the 'Travel Narrative': the obstacles facing those who follow Jesus	Sundays 25-31
SUNDAY 25	'The unjust steward	Lk 16:1-13
SUNDAY 26	'The rich man and Lazarus	Lk 16:19-31
SUNDAY 27	'A lesson on faith and dedication	Lk 17:5-10
SUNDAY 28	'The ten lepers	Lk 17:11-19
SUNDAY 29	'The unjust judge	Lk 18:1-8
SUNDAY 30	'The Pharisee and the tax collector	Lk 18:9-14
SUNDAY 31	'Zacchaeus	Lk 19:1-10
Unit VII	The ministry in Jerusalem	Sundays 32-33
SUNDAY 32	The resurrection debated	Lk 20:27-38
SUNDAY 33	The signs announcing the end	Lk 21:5-19
Unit VIII	Christ the King: reconciliation	Sunday 34
SUNDAY 34	'The repentant thief	Lk 23:35-43

Note: Passages marked with an asterisk are found only in the
Gospel of Luke.

We won't remember what we don't reread: a Catholic schedule of texts.

of chefs, for whereas their works may not themselves erode, the responses of their audiences will. We honour the power of culture but rarely admit with what scandalous ease we forget its individual monuments. Three months after we finish reading a masterpiece, we may struggle to remember a single scene or phrase from it.

Our favourite secular books do not alert us to how inadequate a one-off linear reading of them will prove. They do not identify the particular days of the year on which we ought to reconsider them, as the holy books do – in the latter case with 200 others around us and an organ playing in the background. There is arguably as much wisdom to be found in the stories of Anton Chekhov as in the Gospels, but collections of the former are not bound with calendars reminding readers to schedule a regular review of their insights. We would face grave accusations of eccentricity if we attempted to construct liturgies from the works of secular authors. At best, we haphazardly underline a few of the sentences that we most admire in them and which we may once in a while chance upon in an idle moment waiting for a taxi.

The followers of the faiths feel no such inhibitions. For Jews, the ritual of reading aloud the Five Books of Moses, two sections at a time, on a Monday and a Thursday, has lain at the heart of their religion since the end of the Babylonian captivity in 537 BC. On the twenty-second day of the Hebrew month of Tishrei, the holiday of Simchat Torah marks the end of one read-through of the Books and the start of the next, with the final section of Deuteronomy and the first of Genesis being recited back to back. The congregant who has been assigned to read Deuteronomy 34:1–12 is quaintly designated the *Chatan Torah* ('bridegroom of the Torah'), while the one in charge of reading Genesis 1 is referred to as the *Chatan Bereshit* ('bridegroom of Genesis'). We secular types may think we love books, but how lacklustre our attachment must seem compared with that of the two bridegrooms who make seven circuits around the synagogue, chanting out their joy and beseeching God, '*Hoshiah na*' ('Deliver us') while the other members of the congregation wave flags, kiss one another and shower sweets on all the children present. How regrettable that when we turn the final page of Marcel Proust's *Time Regained*, our own society would consider us peculiar indeed if we went on to compete for the honour of being the bridegroom of *Swann's Way* (*Chatan Bereshit shel betzad shel Swann*).

5.

Secular life is not, of course, unacquainted with calendars and schedules. We know them well in relation to work, and accept the virtues of reminders of lunch meetings, cash-flow projections and tax deadlines. We somehow feel, however, that it would be a violation of our spontaneity to be presented with rotas for rereading Walt Whitman or Marcus Aurelius. Moved though we may be by *Leaves of Grass* or the *Meditations*, we deny that there might be any need, if we wish these books to have a genuine influence on our lives, of revisiting them daily. We are more alarmed by the potentially asphyxiating effects of being compelled to have structured encounters with ideas than by the notion that we might otherwise be in danger of forgetting them altogether.

But forget them we do. The modern world is dense with stimuli, of which none is more insistent than that torrent which we capture with the term 'news'. This entity occupies in the secular sphere much the same position of authority that the liturgical calendar has in the religious one, its main dispatches tracking the canonical hours with uncanny precision: matins have here been transubstantiated into the breakfast bulletin, and vespers into the evening report.

The prestige of the news is founded on the unstated assumption that our lives are forever poised on the verge of critical transformation thanks to the two driving forces of modern history: politics and technology. The earth must therefore be latticed with fibre-optic cables, the waiting rooms of its airports filled with monitors and the public squares of cities ribboned with the chase of stock prices.

For religions, by contrast, there is seldom any need to alter insights or harvest them incrementally through news bulletins. The great stable truths can be written down on vellum or carved into stone rather than swilling malleably across hand-held screens. For 1.6 billion Buddhists, there has been no news of world-altering significance since 483 BC. For their Christian counterparts, the critical events of history came to a close around Easter Sunday in AD 30, while for the Jews the line was drawn a little after the destruction of the Second Temple by the Roman general Titus in AD 70.

Even if we do not concur with the specific messages that religions schedule for us, we can still concede that we have paid a price for our promiscuous involvement with novelty. We occasionally sense the nature of our loss at the end of an evening, as we finally silence the television after watching a report on the opening of a new railway or the tetchy conclusion to a debate over immigration and realize that – in attempting to follow the narrative of man's ambitious progress towards a state of technological and political perfection – we have sacrificed an opportunity to remind ourselves of quieter truths which we know about in theory and forget to live by in practice.

6.

Our peculiar approach to culture spills over from education into associated fields. Comparably suspect assumptions are rife, for example, in the manufacture and sale of books.

Here too we are presented with infinitely more material than we can ever assimilate and we struggle to hold on to what matters most to us. A moderately industrious undergraduate pursuing a degree in the humanities at the beginning of the twenty-first century might run through 800 books before graduation day; by comparison, a wealthy English family in 1250 would have counted itself fortunate to have three books in its possession, this modest library consisting of a Bible, a collection of prayers and a compendium of lives of the saints – these nevertheless costing as much as a cottage. If we lament our book-swamped age, it is because we sense that it is not by reading more, but by deepening and refreshing our understanding of a few volumes that we best develop our intelligence and our sensitivity. We feel guilty for all that we have not yet read, but overlook how much better read we already are than Augustine or Dante, thereby ignoring that our problem lies squarely with our manner of absorption rather than with the extent of our consumption.

We are often urged to celebrate not only that there are so many books to hand, but also that they are so inexpensive. Yet neither of these circumstances should necessarily be deemed unambiguous advantages. The costly and painstaking craftsmanship behind a pre-Gutenberg Bible – revealed in the illuminated flowers in the margins, the naive drawings of Jonah and the whale and the brilliant blue skies dotted with exotic birds above the Virgin – was the product of a society which accepted containment as the basis for immersion, and which wished to elevate individual books into objects of extraordinary beauty so as to emphasize their spiritual and moral significance.

Though technology has rendered it more or less absurd to feel gratitude over owning a book, there remain psychological advantages in rarity. We can revere the care that goes into making a Jewish Sefer Torah, the sacred scroll of the Pentateuch, a copy of which will take a single scribe a year and a half to write out by hand, on a parchment made from the hide of a ceremonially slaughtered goat which has been soaked for nine days in a rabbinically prepared mixture of apple juice, saltwater and gall nuts. We should be prepared to swap a few of our swiftly disintegrating paperbacks for volumes that would proclaim, through the weight and heft of their materials, the grace of their typography and the beauty of their illustrations, our desire for their contents to assume a permanent place in our hearts.

A book which cost as much as a house: an illuminated vellum page from a late-fifteenth-century prayer book, depicting the Adoration of the Magi.

iii. Spiritual Exercises

1.

Alongside setting alternative curricula for universities and emphasizing the need to rehearse and digest knowledge, religions have also been radical in taking education out of the classroom and combining it with other activities, encouraging their followers to learn through all of their senses, not only by listening and reading but also, and more broadly, by *doing*: eating, drinking, bathing, walking and singing.

Zen Buddhism, for instance, proposes ideas about the importance of friendship, the inevitability of frustration and the imperfection of human endeavours. But it does not simply lecture its adherents about these tenets; it helps them more directly to apprehend their truth through activities such as flower arranging, calligraphy, meditation, walking, gravel raking and, most famously, tea drinking.

Because the last of these is at once such a common practice in the West and yet so devoid of spiritual significance, it seems particularly strange as well as delightful that Zen Buddhism should have anointed the tea ceremony as one of its most significant pedagogic moments, as important to Buddhists as the Mass is to Catholics. During *chanoyu*, as the ceremony is known, some of the same feelings that hover faintly over a typical English tea are refined, amplified and symbolically connected to Buddhist doctrine. Every aspect of the ritual has meaning, beginning with the cups, whose misshapen form reflects Zen's affection for all that is raw and unpretentious. The slow way in which the drink is brewed by the tea master allows the demands of the ego to go into abeyance, the simple decorations of the tea hut are meant to draw thoughts away from concerns with status, while the steaming scented tea should help one to feel the truths lurking behind the Chinese characters written on scrolls on the walls denoting key Buddhist virtues like 'harmony', 'purity' and 'tranquillity'.

The point of the tea ceremony is not to teach a new philosophy but to make an existing one more vivid through an activity which carries subtle sympathies with it; it is a mechanism for bringing to life ideas about which participants already have a good intellectual grasp and yet continue to need encouragement to abide by.

To take a comparable example from another faith, Jewish texts make repeated mention of the importance of atonement and the possibilities for renewal through the admission of sin. But within the religion, such ideas are not merely imparted through books, they are made vibrant through a bodily experience: a ritualized version of having a bath. Since the Babylonian exile, Judaism has advised its communities to construct *mikvot* – sacred baths each containing exactly 575 litres of clean spring water – in which Jews are to immerse themselves after confessing to spiritually doubtful acts, in order to recover their purity and their connection to God. The Torah recommends a full immersion in a *mikveh* every Friday afternoon, before the New Year and following every seminal emission.

The institution of the *mikveh* relies on a sense of renewal which secular bathers already know a little about, but lends it greater depth, structure and solemnity. An atheist may, of

A lesson about the meaning of life threaded into a tea party.

course, also feel clean after taking a bath and dirty without one, but the *mikveh* ritual, associating outer hygiene with the recovery of a particular kind of inner purity, like so many other symbolic practices promoted by religions, manages to use a physical activity to support a spiritual lesson.

2.

Religions understand the value of training our minds with a rigour that we are accustomed to applying only to the training of our bodies. They present us with an array of spiritual exercises designed to strengthen our inclination towards virtuous thoughts and patterns of behaviour: they sit us down in unfamiliar spaces, adjust our posture, regulate what we eat, give us scripts detailing what we should say to one another and minutely monitor the thoughts that cross our consciousness. They do all this not in order to deny us freedom but to quell our anxieties and flex our moral capacities.

This double insight – that we should train our minds just as we train our bodies, and that we should do so partly *through* those bodies – has led to the founding, by all the major faiths, of religious retreats where adherents may for a limited time abscond from their ordinary lives and find inner restoration through spiritual exercise.

The secular world offers no true parallels. Our closest equivalents are country hotels and spas, though the comparison serves only to reveal our shallowness. The brochures for such establishments tend to promise us opportunities to rediscover what is most essential to us, they show us images of couples in

Using a bath to support an idea: a Jewish *mikveh* in Willesden,
north-west London.

plush dressing gowns, they vaunt the quality of their mattresses and toiletries or boast of their twenty-four-hour provision of room service. But the emphasis is always on physical satiation and mental diversion rather than on any real fulfilment of the needs of our souls. These places have no way of helping us when the incompatibilities in our relationships reach a new nadir, when reading the Sunday newspapers provokes panic about our careers or when we wake up in terror just before dawn, paralysed by the thought of how short a span of life remains to us. Otherwise solicitous concierges, brimful of ideas about where we might partake of horse riding or mini-golf, will fall suddenly silent when questioned about strategies for coping with guilt, wayward longings or self-loathing.

Religious retreats are, fortunately, somewhat more rounded in their attentions. St Bernard, the founder of the first Cistercian monasteries (organizations which in his day functioned as both retreats for the laity and permanent residences for monks), suggested that all human beings were divided into three parts, *corpus* (body), *animus* (mind) and *spiritus* (spirit), each of which must be carefully looked after by any decent hostelry.

In the tradition of St Bernard, Catholic retreats continue even today to provide their guests with comfortable accommodations, extensive libraries and spiritual activities ranging from the 'examen' – a thrice-daily survey of the conscience, carried out alone and in silence (usually with a lighted candle and a statuette of Jesus) – to sessions with counsellors who have been specially trained to inject logic and morality into believers' confused and corrupted thought processes.

Although the specific lessons taught therein may differ markedly, Buddhist retreats embody an equal commitment to the whole self. After hearing of one in the English countryside specializing in seated and walking forms of meditation, I resolved to see for myself what benefits might be derived from a course of spiritual exercises.

At six in the morning one Saturday in June, some 2,573 years after the Buddha was born not far from Kapilavastu, in the Ganges river basin, I sit in a semicircle with twelve other novices in a converted barn in Suffolk. Our teacher, Tony, begins the session by inviting us to understand the human condition as it is viewed through Buddhist eyes. He says that most of the time, without having any choice in the matter, we are dominated by our ego, or, as it is termed in Sanskrit, our *ātman*. This centre of consciousness is by nature selfish, narcissistic and insatiable, unreconciled to its own mortality and driven to avoid the prospect of death by fantasizing about the redemptive powers of career, status and wealth. It is let loose like a demented dynamo at the moment of our birth and does not incline to rest until we breathe our last. Because the ego is inherently vulnerable, its predominant mood is one of anxiety. It is skittish, jumping from object to object, unable ever to relax its vigilance or engage properly with others. Even under the most auspicious of contexts, it is never far from a relentless, throbbing drumbeat of worry, which conspires to prevent it from sincere involvement with anything outside of itself. And yet the ego also has a touching tendency constantly to trust that its desires are about to be fulfilled. Images of tranquillity

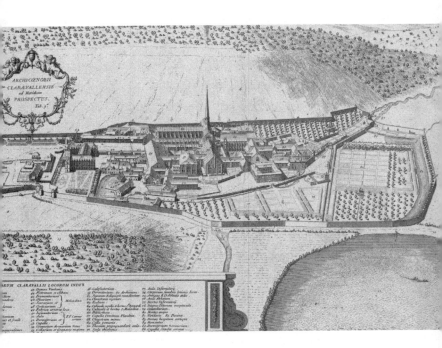

The Cistercian monastery of Clairvaux, 1708: a resting place for the body, mind and spirit. Each zone of the monastery was assigned a different part of the self to heal. The body was to be looked after by the kitchens and the dormitory, the mind by the library and the spirit by the chapel.

and security haunt it: a particular job, social conquest or material acquisition always seems to hold out the promise of an end to craving. In reality, however, each worry will soon enough be replaced by another, and one desire by the next, generating a relentless cycle of what Buddhists call 'grasping', or *upādāna* in Sanskrit.

Nevertheless, as Tony now explains, this sombre picture of one part of ourselves does not have to define all that we are, because we are endowed too with the rare ability, reinforceable through spiritual exercises, occasionally to set aside the demands of our egos and to enter into a state of what Buddhists call *anātman*, or egolessness, during which we can take a step back from our passions and think about what our lives might be like if we were not burdened by the additional and painful need to be ourselves.

It is a sign of the Western bias towards the intellect that it comes as a surprise to be told that we should begin the business of setting aside our egos not primarily through logical argument but rather by learning to sit on the ground in a new way.

As Tony specifies, our capacity to reorient our priorities will critically depend on our ability to stand up, shake our limbs loose for a minute and then rearrange our bodies in the Vairocana seven-point meditation posture. For a group of novices this is, inevitably, something of a struggle, since many of our bodies are no longer quite so young, and all of us seem afflicted by the self-consciousness that naturally results from contorting oneself in one's socks in front of strangers. A certain amount of giggling and even the occasional fart ensue as we strive to imitate Tony's

To answer our longing for calm, Western consumer society has over the last fifty years refined the concept of sunbathing; Buddhism has taken over a thousand years to perfect the art of meditation.

position, which is reputed to be the same one adopted by the Buddha and his disciples as they meditated under a sacred Bodhi tree in the eastern Indian state of Bihar twenty-odd centuries ago. The instructions are precise: our legs must be crossed, our left hand must rest on top of our right in our lap, our spine should be straight, our shoulders lightly stretched, our head inclined forwards, our gaze directed downwards, our mouth slightly open, the tip of our tongue touching the roof of our mouth, our breathing steady and slow.

Gradually the group falls into line, and the room grows silent save for the hoot of an owl in a distant field. Tony guides us to focus on the unremarkable yet rarely remarked-upon fact that we are all breathing. In our first steps towards mastering the *ānāpānasati* ('mindfulness of breathing') meditation, we recognize the extraordinary challenge posed by sitting quietly in a room and doing nothing other than existing – we apprehend, in other words, the draconian grip which the priorities and projects of our egos have on us. We take note of our tendencies towards distraction. As we strive to attend only to our breathing, we sense our conscious minds shooting this way and that on their customarily frantic itineraries. We realize how absurdly difficult we find it to take even three breaths without being seized by an anxiety-charged idea, and extrapolate from that how uncommon it must be for us to inhabit any experience without becoming enmeshed in the tendrils of our *ātman*.

The purpose of our new seating position is to open up a modest distance between our consciousness and our ego. As we feel ourselves breathing, we notice that our physical beings

have rhythms which play out without reference to our ego-led desires. The otherness of the body is one aspect of a vast realm of *anātman* which the ego does not control or understand and to which Buddhism now seeks to introduce us.

Because it is the ego's habit to try to exploit and use as an instrument all that it encounters, it is unaware of the body except in so far as it is useful to its projects for sensory gratification. It is latently resentful of and appalled by its fragility. It does not want to think of the strange ways of the liver or of the mysterious doings of the pancreas. It orders the body to stay faithful to its tasks, hunched over the desk with back muscles clenched into a state of obedience and anxious expectation. Yet now, suddenly, the ego is being asked to cede control to nothing more distinguished and productive than the act of breathing, that background process of inhalation and exhalation which has been going on largely unnoticed and unappreciated since our birth. Taken aback, it experiences some of the same confusion that a king might feel upon being forced, due to unexpected circumstances, to spend a night on a hard bed in a humble inn.

With all our attention directed towards our breathing instead of the ego's demands, it starts to give up some of its claims on consciousness and lets in data which it ordinarily filters out. We become aware of things, both internal and external, that have nothing to do with our usual concerns. Our consciousness shifts from a focus on breathing to an awareness first of our limbs, then of the skeleton that supports us and the blood that is continuously moving within us. We become alive to the sensitivity of our own cheeks, the small stirrings of air in the room, the textures of our clothes against our skin.

Later in the morning, we go outside for another spiritual exercise called a walking meditation, pioneered by the Vietnamese Zen monk Thich Nhat Hanh. We are instructed to empty our minds and wander the landscape without asking anything more of it than to observe it, freed for the moment of those ego-dominated habits of ours which strip nature of its beauty and give us a misleading and troubling sense of our own importance in the cosmos. Under tutelage, we proceed at a camel's pace, our consciousness untroubled by any of our ego's customary ambitions or chidings – in a state as much prized by Buddhism as it is reviled by capitalism, and known in Sanskrit as *apranihita*, or aimlessness – and thereby become newly attuned to a thousand details of our surroundings. There is a shaft of sunlight filtering through the trees, in which minuscule particles of dust are dancing. There is the sound of running water coming from a nearby stream. A spider is making its way across a branch above us. Buddhist poetry is dominated by records of similar encounters with just such tiny facets of the world, which reach our senses only after our egos have loosened their grip on our faculties.

> Coming along the mountain path
> I find something endearing
> about violets

reads a poem by the Zen poet Bashō. Working our way through the undergrowth, we become disinterested surveyors of our own existence, and hence ever so slightly more patient and

compassionate observers of the planet, its people and its small purple flowers.

3.

The specifics of the exercises taught at Buddhist and other retreats are perhaps not as significant as the general point they raise about our need to impose greater discipline on our inner lives.

If the predominant share of our distress is caused by the state of our psyches, it seems perverse that the modern leisure industry should seek always to bring comfort to our bodies without attempting simultaneously to console and tame what the Buddhists so presciently term our 'monkey minds'. We require effective centres for the restoration of our whole beings; new kinds of retreats devoted to educating, through an array of secularized spiritual exercises, our corporeal as well as psychological selves.

iv. Teaching Wisdom

Ultimately, the purpose of all education is to save us time and spare us errors. It is a mechanism whereby society – whether secular or religious – attempts reliably to inculcate in its members, within a set span of years, what it took the very brightest and most determined of their ancestors centuries of painful and sporadic efforts to work out.

Secular society has proved itself ready enough to accept the logic of this mission in relation to scientific and technical knowledge. It sees nothing to regret in the fact that a university student enrolled today on a physics degree will in a matter of months be able to learn as much as Faraday ever knew, and within a couple of years may be pushing at the outer limits of Einstein's unified field theory.

Yet this selfsame principle, which seems at once so obvious and so inoffensive in science, tends to be met with extraordinary opposition when applied to wisdom; to insights related to the self-aware and moral stewardship of the soul. Here, remarkably, the defenders of education, who would ridicule the notion that a class of freshly enrolled physics students ought to be left to work out the theory of electromagnetic radiation on their own, will declaim that wisdom is not something that one person can ever teach another.

This prejudice has so subsumed the teaching of culture as to have more or less stamped out the ambitions of Mill and Arnold, as well as the magniloquent hopes of Rilke, who in the last line of his poem 'Archaic Torso of Apollo' surmised that it was the ultimate wish of all great artists to admonish their audiences, '*Du musst dein Leben ändern*' ('You must change your life').

It is to religions' credit that they have never sided with those who would argue that wisdom is unteachable. They have dared directly to address the great questions of individual life – What should I work for? How do I love? How can I be good? – in ways that should intrigue atheists even if they find little to agree with in the specific answers provided.

As this chapter has suggested, culture is more than adequately equipped to confront our dilemmas without having to rely on religious dogma. The errors that wreak havoc on our personal and political lives have been supplying subject matter for cultural works since antiquity. There is no shortage of information about folly, greed, lust, envy, pride, sentimentality or snobbishness in the canon; all the clues we need can be found in such oeuvres as those of Freud, Marx, Musil, Andrei Tarkovsky, Kenzaburo Oe, Fernando Pessoa, Poussin or Saul Bellow. The problem is that this treasury has seldom been effectively filleted and skilfully served up to us due to unfounded biases against the use of culture in the service of our griefs.

No existing mainstream secular institution has a declared interest in teaching us the art of living. To draw an analogy from the history of science, the ethical field is at the stage of amateurs tinkering with chemicals in garden sheds rather than that of professionals conducting well-structured experiments in research laboratories. University academics, the obvious candidates for any soul-focused pedagogical task, have distanced themselves from demands for relevance by retreating behind a pose of a priori importance. They have shunned the responsibility of seducing their audiences, they have been fatally frightened of simplicity, they have pretended not to notice how fragile we are and they have been blind to how readily we forget everything, however significant it may be.

Religion is laden with ideas for correctives. Its example proposes a new curriculum: a scheme for arranging knowledge according to the challenges to which it relates rather than the academic area in which it happens to fall; a strategy of reading for a purpose (to become better and saner); an investment in oratory and a set of methods for memorizing and more effectively publishing ideas.

In case some of these educational practices should to certain ears sound too *Christian*, we should remember that they frequently far preceded the birth of Jesus. The Greeks and Romans had long been interested in how to calibrate knowledge to inner needs: it was they who first founded schools for disseminating wisdom, compared books to medicines and saw value in rhetoric and repetition. We should not let atheism get in the way of appreciating traditions that are part of a shared non-denominational heritage that was historically stamped out by secularists from a misunderstanding of the real identities of those who had once created it.

Religions do not, as modern universities will, limit their teaching to a fixed period of time (a few years of youth), a particular space (a campus) or a single format (the lecture). Recognizing that we are as much sensory as cognitive creatures, they understand that they will need to use all possible resources to sway our minds. Many of their methods, though remote from contemporary notions of education, should nevertheless be considered essential to any plan to render ideas, be they theological or secular, more effective in our porous minds. These techniques deserve to be studied and adopted, so that we stand a chance of making at least one or two fewer mistakes than the previous generation in the time that remains to us.

V

Tenderness

1.

A fifteenth-century chapel in a backstreet of an unnamed northern European town. It is early afternoon on a sombre winter's day and a middle-aged man shakes down his umbrella and steps inside. The space is warm and dark, lit only by several rows of candles that throw a dance of shadows across the limestone walls. There are comfortable, well-worn pews and, on the floor, prayer cushions, each one embroidered with the words *Mater Dolorosa*. An elderly woman kneels in the far corner, mumbling to herself with her eyes closed.

The man is exhausted. His joints ache. He feels weak, vulnerable and close to tears. No single event has brought him to this point, just a run of minor humiliations that have cumulatively contributed to an overwhelming sense of mediocrity, superfluousness and self-hatred. His career, once so promising, has for a long time now been in descent. He knows how unimpressive he must appear to others, how keen they are to move on from him in social gatherings and just how many of his proposals and letters have gone unanswered. He no longer has the confidence to push himself forward. He is appalled by the seams of impatience and vanity in his character which have led him to this professional impasse. He is stricken by feelings of remorse, foreboding and loneliness. He knows, however, that he couldn't possibly bring these worries home with him. The boys need to believe in his strength. His harried wife has too much on her plate already – and he has learned from experience how badly things turn out when he presents himself to the household in this mood.

He wants to fall asleep and be held. He wants to cry. He wants to be forgiven and reassured. There is music playing through concealed speakers in the chapel, the aria 'Erbarme dich, mein Gott' from Bach's St Matthew Passion. He searches for ideas he can cling to, but nothing seems solid. He is unable to think logically and even making the effort to do so has become more than he can bear.

Having fallen to his knees, he looks up at the painting that hangs above the altar. It shows a tender, sympathetic, gentle young woman with a halo around her head. She gazes back down at him with infinite care – and, without his having to say a word, seems to understand everything.

He remembers the prayers learned so long ago as a child, when he was still thought to be full of potential, when he knew how to make others proud of him, when his parents worried how much he had had to eat and wiped his sticky fingers for him after a meal and when the world and all its opportunities lay before him: 'Holy Mary, Mother of God, pray for us sinners, now and at the hour of our death, Amen.' He closes his eyes and feels the press of tears against his eyelids. 'To you I come; before you I stand, sinful and sorrowful. O Mother of the Word Incarnate, despise not my petitions, but in your mercy hear me and answer me...'

2.

Although we have located this scene in Europe, it could unfold almost anywhere in the world. Comparable moments of despair are to be witnessed every day in the Chapel of Our

Lady of Good Health in Kuala Lumpur and the Shrine of Our Lady of Sorrows in Rhineland, Missouri, in the Grotto of Unyang Dedicated to Our Lady in South Korea and the Nuestra Señora del Espejo in Venezuela. In these sanctuaries the desperate will glance up at the Virgin, light candles, say prayers and speak of their individual griefs to a woman who is not only *Redemptoris Mater*, mother of the redeemer, but also *Mater Ecclesia*, mother of the Church in its entirety and so, symbolically, of all its members.

From a robustly rational perspective, Marian devotion seems to exemplify religion at its most infantile and soft-headed. How could any reasonable adult trust in the existence of a woman who lived several thousand years ago (if she ever lived at all), much less draw comfort from a projected belief in her unblemished heart, her selfless sympathy and her limitless patience?

The drift of the question is hard to refute; it is simply the wrong question to raise. The apposite point is not whether the Virgin exists, but what it tells us about human nature that so many Christians over two millennia have felt the need to invent her. Our focus should be on what the Virgin Mary reveals about our emotional requirements – and, in particular, on what becomes of these demands when we lose our faith.

In the broadest sense, the cult of Mary speaks of the extent to which, despite our adult powers of reasoning, our responsibilities and our status, the needs of childhood endure within us. While for long stretches of our lives we can believe in our maturity, we never succeed in insulating ourselves against the kind of catastrophic events that sweep away our ability to

'I understand': Giovanni Battista Salvi, *The Madonna in Sorrow, c.* 1650.

Prayers to Mary, Vilnius, Lithuania.

reason, our courage and our resourcefulness at putting dramas in perspective and throw us back into a state of primordial helplessness.

At such moments we may long to be held and reassured, as we were decades ago by some sympathetic adult, most likely our mother, a person who made us feel physically protected, stroked our hair, looked at us with benevolence and tenderness and perhaps said not very much other than, very quietly, 'of course'.

Though such longings go largely unmentioned in adult society, it has been the achievement of religions to know how to reanimate and legitimate them. Mary in Christianity, Isis in ancient Egypt, Demeter in Greece, Venus in Rome and Guan Yin in China have all functioned as conduits to recollections of early tenderness. Their statues often stand in darkened, womb-like spaces, their faces are compassionate and supportive, they enable us to sit, talk and cry with them. The similarities between them are too great to be coincidental. We are dealing here with figures that have evolved not out of shared cultural origins but in response to the universal needs of the human psyche.

Chinese Buddhists will visit Guan Yin for the very same reasons that Catholics call on Mary. She too has kind eyes and can suggest alternatives to despising oneself. In temples and outdoor plazas across China, adults allow themselves to be weak in her presence. Her gaze has a habit of making people cry – for the moment one breaks down isn't so much when things are hard as when one finally encounters kindness and a

Guan Yin, Hainan Island, China.

chance to admit to sorrows one has been harbouring in silence for too long. Like Mary, Guan Yin has a sense of the difficulties involved in trying to lead a remotely adequate adult life.

3.

By contrast with religion, atheism is prone to seem coldly impatient with our neediness. The longing for comfort which lies at the heart of the Marian cult seems perilously regressive and at odds with the rational engagement with existence on which atheists pride themselves. Mary and her cohorts have been framed as symptoms of urges which adults ought quickly to outgrow.

At its most withering and intellectually pugnacious, atheism has attacked religion for blinding itself to its own motives, for being unwilling to acknowledge that it is, at base, nothing more than a glorified response to childhood longings which have been dressed up, recast in new forms and projected into the heavens.

This charge may well be correct. The problem is that those who level it are themselves often involved in a denial, a denial of the needs of childhood. In their zeal to attack believers whose frailties have led them to embrace the supernatural, atheists may neglect the frailty that is an inevitable feature of all our lives. They may label as childish particular needs which should really be honoured as more generally human, for there is in truth no maturity without an adequate negotiation with the infantile and no such thing as a grown-up who does not regularly yearn to be comforted like a child.

We can be touched and reassured because this is both us and not us:
Giovanni Bellini, *Madonna and Child*, 1480.

Christianity describes the capacity to accept dependence as a mark of moral and spiritual health. Only the proud and vainglorious would attempt to deny their weaknesses, while the devout can declare without awkwardness, as a sign of their faith, that they have spent time in tears at the foot of a statue of a giant wooden mother. The cult of Mary recasts vulnerability as a virtue and thus corrects our habitual tendency to believe in a conclusive division between adult and childhood selves. At the same time, Christianity is appropriately delicate in the way it frames our needs. It allows us to partake of the comfort of the maternal without forcing us to face up to our lingering and inescapable desire for an actual mother. It makes no mention of *our* mother; it simply offers us the imaginative pleasures of being once again young, babied and cared for by a figure who is *mater* to the world.

4.

If there is a problem with Christianity's approach, it is that it has been *too* successful. The need for comfort has come to be overly identified with a need for Mary herself, instead of being seen for what it really is: an eternal appetite which began long before the Gospels, originating at the very moment when the first child was picked up by his or her mother and soothed amid the darkness and cold of the first underground cave.

That there is no sympathetic mother or caring father out there who can make everything all right for us is no reason to deny how strongly we wish that there could be. Religion teaches us to be gentle on ourselves in those times of crisis when, desperate and afraid, we confusedly cry out for help from *someone* – even though we ostensibly don't believe in anything, even though our own mother is long dead, our father was unavailable and cruel and we now occupy a responsible and grown-up place in the world.

The example of Catholicism suggests that art and architecture have a role to play at such times, for it is through looking at images of parental faces turned lovingly towards children, usually in the quiet, darkened recesses of chapels, museums and associated places of veneration, that we sense some primordial need in us being answered and a certain balance restored.

It would be useful if our secular artists were occasionally to create works which took parental care as their central theme, and if architects designed spaces, whether in museums or, more ambitiously, in new Temples to Tenderness, where we could contemplate these new works in a twilight ambience.

The Marian cult dares to propose to all atheists, even the most hard-headed, that they too remain vulnerable and pre-rational in their hearts, and might learn to help themselves out of certain darker moods through an accommodation with their eternally artless and immature sides.

In rejecting superstition, we should take care that we aren't tempted to ignore the less respectable longings which religions have been so successful in identifying and dignified in resolving.

Adult life isn't possible without moments when, with reason being ineffective, all we can do is *regress*. A secular Temple to Tenderness, backlit by Mary Cassatt's 1893 painting *The Child's Bath*.

VI

Pessimism

1.

Christianity has spent much of its history emphasizing the darker side of earthly existence. Yet even within this sombre tradition, the French philosopher Blaise Pascal stands out for the exceptionally merciless nature of his pessimism. In his *Pensées*, written between 1658 and 1662, Pascal misses no opportunity to confront his readers with evidence of mankind's resolutely deviant, pitiful and unworthy nature. In seductive classical French, he informs us that happiness is an illusion ('Anyone who does not see the vanity of the world is very vain himself'), that misery is the norm ('If our condition were truly happy we should not need to divert ourselves from thinking about it'), that true love is a chimera ('How hollow and foul is the heart of man'), that we are as thin-skinned as we are vain ('A trifle consoles us because a trifle upsets us'), that even the strongest among us are rendered helpless by the countless diseases to which we are vulnerable ('Flies are so mighty that they can paralyse our minds and eat up our bodies'), that all worldly institutions are corrupt ('Nothing is surer than that people will be weak') and that we are absurdly prone to overestimate our own importance ('How many kingdoms know nothing of us!'). The very best we may hope to do in these circumstances, he suggests, is to face the desperate facts of our situation head-on: 'Man's greatness comes from knowing he is wretched.'

Given the tone, it comes as something of a surprise to discover that reading Pascal is not at all the depressing experience one might have presumed. The work is consoling, heartwarming and even, at times, hilarious. For those teetering on the verge of despair, there can paradoxically be no finer book to turn to than one which seeks to grind man's every last hope into the dust. The *Pensées*, far more than any saccharine volume touting inner beauty, positive thinking or the realization of hidden potential, has the power to coax the suicidal off the ledge of a high parapet.

If Pascal's pessimism can effectively console us, it may be because we are usually cast into gloom not so much by negativity as by hope. It is hope – with regard to our careers, our love lives, our children, our politicians and our planet – that is primarily to blame for angering and embittering us. The incompatibility between the grandeur of our aspirations and the mean reality of our condition generates the violent disappointments which rack our days and etch themselves in lines of acrimony across our faces.

Hence the relief, which can explode into bursts of laughter, when we finally come across an author generous enough to confirm that our very worst insights, far from being unique and shameful, are part of the common, inevitable reality of mankind. Our dread that we might be the only ones to feel anxious, bored, jealous, cruel, perverse and narcissistic turns out to be gloriously unfounded, opening up unexpected opportunities for communion around our dark realities.

We should honour Pascal, and the long line of Christian pessimists to which he belongs, for doing us the incalculably great favour of publicly and elegantly rehearsing the facts of our sinful and pitiful state.

2.

This is not a stance for which the modern world betrays much sympathy, for one of this world's dominant characteristics, and certainly its greatest flaw, is its optimism.

Despite occasional moments of panic, most often connected to market crises, wars or pandemics, the secular age maintains an all but irrational devotion to a narrative of improvement, based on a messianic faith in the three great drivers of change: science, technology and commerce. Material improvements since the mid-eighteenth century have been so remarkable, and have so exponentially increased our comfort, safety, wealth and power, as to deal an almost fatal blow to our capacity to remain pessimistic – and therefore, crucially, to our ability to stay sane and content. It has been impossible to hold on to a balanced assessment of what life is likely to provide for us when we have witnessed the cracking of the genetic code, the invention of the mobile phone, the opening of Western-style supermarkets in remote corners of China and the launch of the Hubble telescope.

Yet while it is undeniable that the scientific and economic trajectories of mankind have been pointed firmly in an upward direction for several centuries, *we* do not comprise mankind: none of us individuals can dwell exclusively amidst the ground-breaking developments in genetics or telecommunications that lend our age its distinctive and buoyant prejudices. We may derive some benefit from the availability of hot baths and computer chips, but our lives are no less subject to accident, frustrated ambition, heartbreak, jealousy, anxiety or death than were those of our medieval forebears. But at least our ancestors had the advantage of living in a religious era which never made the mistake of promising its population that happiness could ever make a permanent home for itself on this earth.

3.

Christianity is not, in and of itself, an unhopeful institution. It merely has the good sense to locate its expectations firmly in the next life, in the moral and material perfection of a world far beyond this one.

This relegation of hope to a distant sphere has enabled the Church to be uniquely clear-eyed and unsentimental about earthly reality. It does not assume that politics could ever create perfect justice, that any marriage could be free of conflict or dissent, that money could ever deliver security, that a friend could be unfailingly loyal or, more generally, that Heavenly Jerusalem could be built on ordinary ground. Since its founding, the religion has maintained a usefully sober vision, of a kind that the secular world has been too sentimental and cowardly to embrace, about our chances of improving on the brute facts of our corrupted natures.

The secular are at this moment in history a great deal more optimistic than the religious – something of an irony, given the frequency with which the latter have been derided by the former for their apparent naivety and credulousness. It is the secular whose longing for perfection has grown so intense as to lead them to imagine that paradise might be realized on this earth after just a few more years of financial growth and medical

We would be wise to locate ideas of perfection in another world altogether:
Jan Brueghel the Younger, *Paradise*, *c.* 1620.

research. With no evident awareness of the contradiction they may, in the same breath, gruffly dismiss a belief in angels while sincerely trusting that the combined powers of the IMF, the medical research establishment, Silicon Valley and democratic politics could together cure the ills of mankind.

4.

It is the most ambitious and driven among us who are the most sorely in need of having our reckless hopes dampened through immersive dousings in the darkness which religions have explored. This is a particular priority for secular Americans, perhaps the most anxious and disappointed people on earth, for their nation infuses them with the most extreme hopes about what they may be able to achieve in their working lives and relationships. We should cease to view the pessimism of religions as belonging to them alone, or as indelibly dependent on hopes for salvation. We should strive to adopt the acute perspective of those who believe in paradise, even as we live out our own lives abiding by the fundamental atheistic precept that this is the one world we will ever know.

5.

The benefits of a philosophy of neo-religious pessimism are nowhere more apparent than in relation to marriage, one of modern society's most grief-stricken arrangements, which has been rendered unnecessarily hellish by the astonishing secular supposition that it should be entered into principally for the sake of happiness.

Christian and Jewish marriages, while not always jovial, are at least spared the second order of suffering which arises from the mistaken impression that it is somehow wrong or unjust to be malcontent. Christianity and Judaism present marriage not as a union inspired and governed by subjective enthusiasm but rather, and more modestly, as a mechanism by which individuals can assume an adult position in society and thence, with the help of a close friend, undertake to nurture and educate the next generation under divine guidance. These limited expectations tend to forestall the suspicion, so familiar to secular partners, that there might have been more intense, angelic or less fraught alternatives available elsewhere. Within the religious ideal, friction, disputes and boredom are signs not of error, but of life proceeding according to plan.

Notwithstanding their practical approach, these religions do recognize our desire to adore passionately. They know of our need to believe in others, to worship and serve them and to find in them a perfection which eludes us in ourselves. They simply insist that these objects of adoration should always be divine rather than human. Therefore they assign us eternally youthful, attractive and virtuous deities to shepherd us through life, while reminding us on a daily basis that human beings are comparatively humdrum and flawed creations worthy of forgiveness and patience, a detail which is apt to elude our notice in the heat of marital squabbling. 'Why can't you be more perfect?' is the incensed question that lurks beneath a majority of secular arguments. In their effort to keep us from hurling our curdled dreams at one another,

The faiths have the good sense to provide us with angels to worship and lovers to tolerate.

the faiths have the good sense to provide us with angels to worship and lovers to tolerate.

6.

A pessimistic worldview does not have to entail a life stripped of joy. Pessimists can have a far greater capacity for appreciation than their opposite numbers, for they never expect things to turn out well and so may be amazed by the modest successes which occasionally break across their darkened horizons. Modern secular optimists, on the other hand, with their well-developed sense of entitlement, generally fail to savour any epiphanies of everyday life as they busy themselves with the construction of earthly paradise.

Accepting that existence is inherently frustrating, that we are forever hemmed in by atrocious realities, can give us the impetus to say 'Thank you' a little more often. It is telling that the secular world is not well versed in the art of gratitude: we no longer offer up thanks for harvests, meals, bees or clement weather. On a superficial level, we might suppose that this is because there is no one to say 'Thank you' *to*. But at base it seems more a matter of ambition and expectation. Many of those blessings for which our pious and pessimistic ancestors offered thanks, we now pride ourselves on having worked hard enough to take for granted. Is there really any need, we wonder, to carve out a moment of gratitude in honour of a sunset or an apricot? Are there not loftier goals towards which we might be aiming?

Seeking to induct us in a contrary attitude of humility, the Jewish Prayer Book of the United Congregation commends a specific prayer to be said on the occasion of 'eating a seasonal fruit for the first time in the year', and another to mark the acquisition of 'a new garment of significant value'. It even includes a prayer intended to prompt admiration for the complexity of the human digestive system:

> 'Blessed are You, Lord our God, King of the Universe, who formed man in wisdom and created in him many orifices and cavities.
>
> It is revealed and known before the throne of Your glory that were one of them to be ruptured or blocked, it would be impossible to survive and stand before You.
>
> Blessed are You, Lord, Healer of all flesh, who does wondrous deeds.'

7.

Religions have wisely insisted that we are inherently flawed creatures: incapable of lasting happiness, beset by troubling sexual desires, obsessed by status, vulnerable to appalling accidents and always slowly dying.

They have also, of course, in many cases believed in the possibility that a deity might be able to help us. We see this combination of despair and hope with particular clarity at Jerusalem's Western or Wailing Wall, where Jews have, since the second half of the sixteenth century, gathered to air their griefs and to beg their creator for help. At the base of the wall, they have

The Wailing Wall, Jerusalem.

written down their sorrows on small pieces of paper, inserted these into gaps among the stones and hoped that God would be moved to mercy by their pain.

Remove God from this equation and what do we have left? Bellowing humans calling out in vain to an empty sky. This is tragic and yet, if we are to rescue a shred of comfort from the bleakness, at least the dejected are to be found weeping *together*. Only too often, in bed late at night, we panic at sorrows which seem devilishly unique to us. No such illusions are possible at the Wailing Wall. It is clear that the whole race is forlorn. The Wall marks out a locus where the anguish we otherwise bear silently within us can be revealed for what it truly is: merely a thimbleful of sorrow in an ocean of suffering. It serves to reassure us of the ubiquity of disaster and definitively corrects the smiling assumptions unwittingly made by contemporary culture.

Among the advertisements for jeans and computers high above the streets of our cities, we should place electronic versions of Wailing Walls that would anonymously broadcast our inner woes, and thereby give us all a clearer sense of what is involved in being alive. Such walls would be particularly consoling were they able to afford us a glimpse of what is in Jerusalem reserved only for the eyes of God: the particulars of the misfortunes of others, the details of the broken hearts, dashed ambitions, sexual fiascos, jealous stalemates and ruinous bankruptcies that normally remain hidden behind our impassive fronts. Such walls would lend us reassuring proofs that others too were worrying about their absurdity, counting how few summers they had left, crying over someone who abandoned them a decade ago and dynamiting their chances of success through idiocy and impatience. There would be no resolutions on offer in these venues, no end to suffering, only a basic – and yet infinitely comforting – public acknowledgement that we are none of us alone in the extent of our troubles and our lamentations.

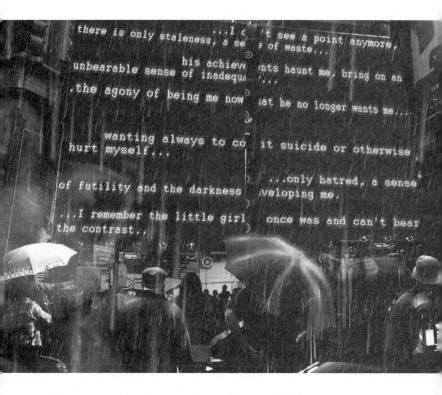

there is only staleness, a se...I c 't see a point anymore, of waste...

unbearable sense his achievents haunt me, bring on an of inadequ...

.the agony of being me now at he no longer wants me....

wanting always to co it suicide or otherwise
hurt myself...

of futility and the darkness ...only hatred, a sense veloping me.

...I remember the little girl once was and can't bear the contrast..

The gravest problems have no solutions, but it would help never again to have to labour under the illusion that we had been singled out for persecution.

VII

Perspective

1.

For atheists, one of the most consoling texts of the Old
Testament should be the Book of Job, which concerns itself
with the theme of why bad things happen to good people – a
question to which, intriguingly, it refuses to offer up simple,
faith-based answers. Instead it suggests that it is not for us to
know why events occur in the way they do, that we should not
always interpret pain as punishment and that we should recall
that we live in a universe riddled with mysteries, of which the
vagaries in our fortunes are certainly not the largest or even,
as we will become aware if only we can look at matters from a
sufficient remove, among the most important.

The Book of Job begins by introducing us to its eponymous
hero, a man from Uz, on whom God appears to have bestowed
every imaginable favour. When we first meet him, Job is living
in a large house, he is virtuous and content, he has seven sons
and three daughters, 7,000 sheep, 3,000 camels, 500 yoke of
oxen and 500 donkeys. Then, in a single day, a catastrophic
series of disasters befall him, his family and his livestock. First a
band of violent Sabaeans make off with the oxen and donkeys.
Then a great storm breaks out and lightning kills every last one
of the sheep. Members of a neighbouring tribe, the Chaldeans,
steal the camels. Worst of all, a hurricane blows in from the
desert and destroys the house of Job's eldest son, killing the
youth and all of his nine siblings, who have gathered inside for
a feast.

As if these tribulations were not enough, mysterious sores
begin to spread over Job's body, rendering his every least

movement excruciating. Sitting in a pile of ashes, a broken man, Job scrapes at his skin with a shard of pottery and, in terror and sorrow, asks God why all of these things have happened to him.

Job's friends think they know the answer: he must have sinned. Bildad the Shuhite is certain that God would not have killed Job's children had they – and Job himself – not done something very wrong. 'God will not reject a righteous man,' Bildad confides. Zophar the Naamathite goes so far as to hint that Job's crimes must have been terrible indeed, and God generous in his treatment of him, because the Lord always forgives more than he punishes.

Job dismisses these explanations, though, as nothing more than 'proverbs of ashes' and 'defences of clay'. He knows that he has not sinned. Why, then, has he been beset by these troubles? Why has God forsaken him? Does God even exist?

At last, after a good deal of further debate among the men, Yahweh himself is prompted to answer Job. From a whirlwind in the desert, furious, God thunders:

> 'Who is this that darkeneth counsel by words
> without knowledge?
>
> Gird up now thy loins like a man; for I will demand
> of thee …
>
> Where wast thou when I laid
> the foundations of the earth? declare, if thou has
> understanding …
>
> By what way is the light parted, which scattereth
> the east wind upon the earth? …

> Out of whose womb came the ice? and the hoary
> frost of heaven ... ? ...
> Knowest thou the ordinances of heaven? ...
> Doth the hawk fly by thy wisdom ... ? ...
> Canst thou draw out leviathan with an hook?'

Job's direct challenge regarding God's existence and ethical intentions is thus met with an indirect response, wherein the deity goes on at length about how little humans know of anything. Fragile, limited creatures that they are, how can they possibly understand the ways of God? he demands. And given their ignorance, what right do they have to use such words as *undeserved* and *unmerited*? There are untold things about the galaxy that mankind cannot properly interpret and upon which, therefore, it ought not presume to impose its flawed logic. Human beings did not bring the cosmos into being and, despite their occasional feelings to the contrary, they do not control or own it. God tries to shake Job out of his preoccupation with the events in his own life by drawing his attention to the immensity and variety of nature. He evokes a sweeping vision of the totality of existence, from the foundation of the earth to the tracks of the constellations, from the heights attained by a hawk in flight to the labour pains of a mountain goat, in the hope of instilling in the man from Uz a redeeming sense of awe.

The strategy works: Job is reminded of the scale of all that surpasses him and of the age, size and mystery of space. God's whirlwind, and the sonorous, sublime words he speaks, excite a pleasing terror in his audience, a sense of how petty are man's disasters in comparison with the ways of eternity, leaving Job – and the rest of us, perhaps – a little readier to bow to the incomprehensible and morally obscure tragedies that every life entails.

2.

Some millennia after Job received his lesson from God, another Jew, Benedictus de Spinoza, undertook to reframe the same argument in a more secular idiom.

Spinoza had no patience with the notion of an anthropomorphic Supreme Being who could speak to his followers from a mountaintop and dwelt in the clouds. For him, 'God' was merely a scientific term for the force that had created the universe, the first cause or, in the philosopher's preferred phrase, the 'cause of itself', *causa sui*.

As a philosophical construct, this God offered Spinoza considerable consolation. During moments of frustration and disaster, the philosopher recommended the adoption of a cosmic perspective, or a re-envisioning of the situation, in his famous and lyrical coinage, 'under the aspect of eternity', *sub specie aeternitatis*. Fascinated by the new technology of his age – and most of all by telescopes and the knowledge they yielded of other planets – Spinoza proposed that we use our imaginations to step outside ourselves and practise submitting our will to the laws of the universe, however contrary these might seem to our intentions.

We are not so very far, here, from God's advice to Job: rather than try to redress our humiliations by insisting on our wronged importance, we should instead endeavour to apprehend and appreciate our essential nothingness. The signal danger of life in a godless society is that it lacks reminders of the transcendent and therefore leaves us unprepared for disappointment and eventual annihilation. When God is dead, human beings – much to their detriment – are at risk of taking psychological centre stage. They imagine themselves to be commanders of their own destinies, they trample upon nature, forget the rhythms of the earth, deny death and shy away from valuing and honouring all that slips through their grasp, until at last they must collide catastrophically with the sharp edges of reality.

Our secular world is lacking in the sorts of rituals that might put us gently in our place. It surreptitiously invites us to think of the present moment as the summit of history, and the achievements of our fellow humans as the measure of all things – a grandiosity that plunges us into continuous swirls of anxiety and envy.

3.

Religion is above all a symbol of what exceeds us and an education in the advantages of recognizing our paltriness. It has natural sympathies with all those aspects of existence which decentre us: glaciers, oceans, microscopic life forms, newborn babies or the resonant language of Milton's *Paradise Lost* ('Floods and Whirlwinds of tempestuous fire ...'). Being put in our place by something larger, older, greater than ourselves is not a humiliation; it should be accepted as a relief from our insanely hopeful ambitions for our lives.

Religion is more acute than philosophy in understanding that it is not enough merely to sketch out such ideas in books. It would of course be ideal if we could – faithful and faithless alike – view things *sub specie aeternitatis* at all times, but we are almost certain to fall out of the habit unless we are firmly and consistently reminded to do so.

Among the cannier initiatives of religion, then, has been the provision of regular souvenirs of the transcendent, at morning prayer and the weekly service, at the harvest festival and the baptism, on Yom Kippur and on Palm Sunday. The secular world is lacking an equivalent cycle of moments during which we, too, might be prodded to imaginatively step out of the earthly city and recalibrate our lives according to a larger and more cosmic set of measurements.

If such a process of re-evaluation offers any common point of access open to both atheists and believers, it may be via an element in nature which is mentioned in both the Book of Job and Spinoza's *Ethics*: the stars. It is through their contemplation that the secular are afforded the best chance of experiencing redemptive feelings of awe.

Myopically, the scientific authorities who are officially in charge of interpreting the stars for the rest of us seem rarely to recognize the therapeutic import of their subject matter. In austere scientific language, the space agencies inform us of the properties and paths of the heavenly bodies, yet they seldom consider astronomy as either a source of wisdom or a plausible corrective to suffering.

Science should matter to us not only because it helps us to control parts of the world, but also because it shows us things that we will *never* master. Thus we would do well to meditate daily, rather as the religious do on their God, on the 9.5 trillion kilometres which comprise a single light year, or perhaps on the luminosity of the largest known star in our galaxy, Eta Carinae, 7,500 light years distant, 400 times the size of the sun and 4 million times as bright. We should punctuate our calendars with celebrations in honour of VY Canis Majoris, a red hypergiant in the constellation Canis Major, 5,000 light years from earth and 2,100 times bigger than our sun. Nightly – perhaps after the main news bulletin and before the celebrity quiz – we might observe a moment of silence in order to contemplate the 200 to 400 billion stars in our galaxy, the 100 billion galaxies and the 3 septillion stars in the universe. Whatever their value may be to science, the stars are in the end no less valuable to mankind as solutions to our megalomania, self-pity and anxiety.

To answer our need to be repeatedly connected through our senses to ideas of transcendence, we should insist that a percentage of all prominently positioned television screens on public view be hooked up to live feeds from the transponders of our extraplanetary telescopes.

We would then be able to ensure that our frustrations, our broken hearts, our hatred of those who haven't called us and our regrets over opportunities that have passed us by would continuously be rubbed up against, and salved by, images of galaxies such as Messier 101, a spiral structure which sits towards the bottom left corner of the constellation Ursa Major, 23 million light years away, majestically unaware of everything we are and consolingly unaffected by all that tears us apart.

Piccadilly Circus, the Messier 101 galaxy, part of the constellation Ursa Major, via the Hubble telescope.

VIII

Art

1.

For some atheists, one of the most difficult aspects of renouncing religion is having to give up on ecclesiastical art and all the beauty and emotion therein. However, to voice regret over this in the presence of many non-believers is to run the risk of being rebuked for sentimental nostalgia and then, perhaps, brusquely reminded that secular societies have in any case developed their own, highly effective means of satisfying the artistic appetites once fed by the faiths.

These non-believers are likely to point out that even where we no longer put up churches, we are still drawn to construct grand buildings that celebrate our visual ideals. The best architects vie for the chance to design these structures; they dominate our cities; they attract pilgrims from all over the world and our voices instinctively drop to a whisper the moment we enter their awe-inspiring galleries. Hence the analogy so often drawn: our museums of art have become our new churches.

The argument has an immediate and seductive plausibility to it. The similarities seem incontrovertible. Like churches, museums enjoy an unparalleled status: they are where we might take a group of visiting aliens to show them what we most delight in and revere. Like churches, they are also the institutions to which the wealthy most readily donate their surplus capital – in the hope of cleansing themselves of whatever sins they may have racked up in the course of accumulating it. Moreover, time spent in museums seems to confer some of the same psychological benefits as attendance at church services; we experience comparable feelings of communing with something greater than ourselves and of being separated from the compromised and profane world beyond. We may even get a little bored sometimes, as we would in churches, but we emerge with a sense that we have, in a variety of indeterminate ways, become slightly better people.

Like universities, museums promise to fill the gaps left by the ebbing of faith; they too stand to give us meaning without superstition. Just as secular books hold out a hope that they can replace the Gospels, so museums may be able to take over the aesthetic responsibilities of churches.

2.

However beguiling this thesis sounds, it suffers from some of the same flaws that bedevil the corresponding argument about the teaching of culture within universities. Museums may in theory be well equipped to satisfy needs formerly catered to by religion, but, rather like universities, in practice they abdicate much of their potential through the way they handle the precious material entrusted to them. While exposing us to objects of genuine importance, they nevertheless seem incapable of adequately linking these to the needs of our souls. We are too often looking at the right pictures through the wrong frames. Yet if there is cause for optimism, it relates to another similarity between museums and universities: both institutions are open to having some of their more uncertain assumptions illuminated through the insights of religion.

The fundamental question which the modern museum has unusual but telling difficulty in answering is why art should matter. It vociferously insists on art's significance and rallies governments, donors and visitors accordingly. But it subsequently retreats into a curious, institutional silence about what this importance might actually be based on. We are left feeling as though we must have missed out on crucial stages of an argument which the museum has in reality never made, beyond trailing a tautological contention that art should matter to us because it is so important.

As a result, we tend to enter galleries with grave, though by necessity discreet, doubts about what we are meant to do in them. What we must of course never do is treat works of art *religiously*, especially if (as is often the case) they happen to be religious in origin. The modern museum is no place for visitors to get on their knees before once-sacred objects, weep and beg for reassurance and guidance. In many countries museums were explicitly founded as new, secular environments in which religious art could (in contravention of the wishes of its makers) be seen stripped of its theological context. It was no coincidence that during the period of revolutionary government in France in 1792, only three days separated the declaration of the state's official severance from the Catholic Church and the inauguration of the Palais du Louvre as the country's first national museum. The Louvre's galleries were quickly filled with items looted from French Catholic churches, and subsequently, thanks to Napoleon's campaigns, from monasteries and chapels across Europe.

What we can no longer pray to, we are now generally invited to garner facts about. Being an art 'expert' is associated

What should we do with her when we can't pray to her? *Virgin and Child, c.* 1324, confiscated from the Abbey of Saint-Denis, Paris, in 1789.

It can be so hard not to think of the cafeteria: Thomas Struth,
National Gallery I, London 1989.

primarily with knowing a great deal: about where a work was made, who paid for it, where its artist's parents came from and what his or her artistic influences may have been.

In a cabinet in one of the medieval galleries of the Louvre we find a statuette identified as *Virgin and Child*, stolen from the Abbey of Saint-Denis in 1789. For centuries before its relegation to the museum, people regularly knelt before it and drew strength from Mary's compassion and serenity. However, to judge by its caption and catalogue entry, in the view of the modern Louvre, what we really need to do with it is *understand* it – understand that it is made of gilded silver, that in her free hand Mary holds a crystal fleur-de-lis, that the piece is typical of Parisian metalwork fabricated in the first half of the fourteenth century, that the figure's overall shape derives from that of a Byzantine model called the *Virgin of Tenderness* and that this is the earliest dated French example of the translucent *basse-taille* enamelwork first developed by Tuscan craftsmen in the late thirteenth century.

Unfortunately, when it is presented to us principally as a storehouse of concrete information, art soon starts to lose its interest for all but a determined few. A measure of this indifference emerges from a series of images by the German photographer Thomas Struth which shows us tourists making their way around some of the world's great museums. Patently unable to draw much sustenance from their surroundings, they stand bemused in front of *Annunciation*s and *Crucifixion*s, dutifully consulting their catalogues, perhaps taking in the date of a work or an artist's name, while before them a line

What might we do in front of this? Fiona Banner, *Every Word Unmade*, 2007.

of crimson blood trickles down the muscular leg of the son of God or a dove hovers in a cerulean sky. They appear to want to be transformed by art, but the lightning bolts they are waiting for seem never to strike. They resemble the disappointed participants in a failed seance.

The puzzlement shared by museum-goers only increases when we turn to the art of our own era. We look at a giant neon version of the alphabet. We take in a vat of gelatinous water in which a sheet of aluminium fixed to a motor is swaying back and forth to the amplified sound of a human heartbeat. We watch a grainy film of an elderly woman slicing an apple, intercut with footage of a lion running across a savannah. And we think to ourselves that only an idiot or a reactionary would dare to ask what all this could mean. The only certainty is that neither the artist nor the museum is going to help us: wall texts are kept to a minimum; catalogues are enigmatically written. It would take a brave soul to raise a hand.

3.

Christianity, by contrast, never leaves us in any doubt about what art is for: it is a medium to remind us about what matters. It exists to guide us to what we should worship and revile if we wish to be sane, good people in possession of well-ordered souls. It is a mechanism whereby our memories are forcibly jogged about what we have to love and to be grateful for, as well as what we should draw away from and be afraid of.

The German philosopher Hegel defined art as 'the sensuous presentation of ideas'. It is, he indicated, in the business of

Art is the sensuous presentation of ideas crucial to the health of our souls. Here, a reminder of love. *Top*: Filippino Lippi, *The Adoration of the Child,* early 1480s. *Above*: Audrey Bardou, grandparents with their grandchildren, 2008.

conveying concepts, just like ordinary language, except that it engages us through both our senses *and* our reason, and is uniquely effective for its dual modes of address.

To return to one of the familiar themes of this book, we need art because we are so forgetful. We are creatures of the body as well as of the mind, and so require art to stir our languid imaginations and motivate us in ways that mere philosophical expositions cannot. Many of our most important ideas get flattened and overlooked in everyday life, their truth rubbed off through casual use. We know intellectually that we should be kind and forgiving and empathetic, but such adjectives have a tendency to lose all their meaning until we meet with a work of art that grabs us through our senses and won't let us go until we have properly remembered why these qualities matter and how badly society needs them for its balance and its sanity. Even the word *love* has a habit of growing sterile and banal in the abstract, until the moment when we glimpse a contemporary photograph of two grandparents patiently feeding their grandchildren an apple purée for supper, or a fifteenth-century rendering of Mary and her son at nap-time – and remember why love lies at the core of our humanity

We might modify Hegel's definition to bring it more fully into line with Christianity's insights: good art is the sensuous presentation of those ideas which matter most to the proper functioning of our souls – and yet which we are most inclined to forget, even though they are the basis for our capacity for contentment and virtue.

A role for art at key moments of life: *tavolette*.

Christianity was never troubled by the notion of charging art with an educative, therapeutic mission. Its own art willingly aspired to the status of propaganda. Although the noun has become one of the more frightening in our lexicon, coloured by the sinister ends towards which certain historical regimes have put it to work, propaganda is a neutral concept in its essence, suggesting merely influence rather than any particular direction for it. We may associate propaganda with corruption and tasteless posters, but Christianity took it to be synonymous with the artistic enhancement of our receptivity to such qualities as modesty, friendship and courage.

From the fourteenth century to the end of the nineteenth, a brotherhood in Rome was renowned for tracking down prisoners on their way to the gallows and placing before their eyes *tavolette*, or small boards bearing images from the Christian story – usually of Christ on the Cross or the Virgin and Child – in the hope that these representations would bring the condemned solace in their final minutes. It is difficult to conceive of a more extreme example of a belief in the redemptive capacity of images, and yet the brotherhood was only carrying out a mission to which Christian art has always been committed: that of putting examples of the most important ideas in front of us at difficult moments, to help us to live and to die.

4.

Among these important ideas, none has been more significant to Christianity than the notion of suffering. We are all, in the religion's eyes, inherently vulnerable beings who will not get

So that we should all know what suffering is like, realize that none of us will escape it and grow kinder through this recognition: Matthias Grünewald, Isenheim Altarpiece, 1516.

through life without meeting with atrocious griefs of mind and body. Christianity also knows that any pain is aggravated by a sense that we are alone in experiencing it. However, we are as a rule not very skilled at communicating the texture of our troubles to others, or at sensing the sorrows they themselves are hiding behind stoic façades. We are therefore in need of art to help us to understand our own neglected hurt, to grasp everything that does not come up in casual conversation and to coax us out of an unproductively isolated relationship with our most despised and awkward qualities.

For a thousand years and more, Christian artists have been directing their energies towards making us feel what it would be like to have large, rusty nails hammered into our palms, to bleed from weeping wounds in our sides and to climb a steep hill on legs already broken by the weight of the cross we are carrying. The depiction of such pain is not meant to be ghoulish; rather, it is intended to be a route to moral and psychological development, a way to increase our feelings of solidarity as well as our capacities for compassion.

In the spring of 1512, Matthias Grünewald began work on an altarpiece for the Monastery of St Anthony in Isenheim, in north-eastern France. The monks of this order specialized in tending to the sick, and most particularly to those afflicted with ergotism, or St Anthony's fire, a usually fatal disease which causes seizures, hallucinations and gangrene. Once the work was ready, it became customary for patients, on their arrival at the monastery, to be taken to the chapel to see it, so that they might understand that in the suffering they were now enduring, they had once been equalled, and perhaps exceeded, by God's own son.

It is fundamental to the power of the Christian story that Jesus died in more or less the greatest agony ever experienced by anyone. He thus offers all human beings, however racked by illness and grief, evidence that they are not alone in their condition – sparing them, if not suffering itself, then at least the defeated feeling that they have been singled out for unusual punishment.

Jesus's story is a register of pain – betrayal, loneliness, self-doubt, torture – through which our own anguish can be mirrored and contextualized, and our impressions of its rarity corrected. Such impressions are of course not hard to form, given how vigorously society waves away our difficulties and surrounds us with sentimental commercial images which menace us by seeming so far removed from our reality in their promises.

Christianity recognizes the capacity of the best art to give shape to pain and thereby to attenuate the worst of our feelings of paranoia and isolation. Catholic artists have long been in the habit of producing cycles of paintings known as the Seven Sorrows of Mary, renderings of the most painful episodes in the life of the Virgin, from the prophecy of Simeon to Jesus's death and burial. Tradition dictates that the faithful should meditate on these works and endeavour through them to better understand not only Mary's trials but also those endured by mothers more generally. The underlying intention of these Marian cycles, although they were defined by the particularities of Catholicism, could nevertheless be a source of inspiration for atheists. We might consider setting contemporary artists

Bernard van Orley and Pedro Campana,
The Seven Sorrows of the Virgin (detail),
c. 1520–35.

Art attenuates the feeling of being beyond understanding: an image by François
Coquerel, from an imagined cycle of the Twelve Sorrows of Adolescence.

the task of depicting a Seven Sorrows of Parenthood, a Twelve Sorrows of Adolescence or a Twenty-one Sorrows of Divorce.

The most famous of all Catholic cycles of suffering is the Fourteen Stations of the Cross, whose elements illustrate the tragic final chapter of Jesus's life, beginning with the Condemnation and ending with the Laying in the Tomb. Hung in order around the niches or columns of a church, the Stations are meant to be toured in an anticlockwise itinerary, with each stage throwing light on a different aspect of agony.

While Jesus's end may have been exceptionally barbarous, the strategy of organizing a cycle of representative images of difficulty, of enriching these with commentaries and hanging them in an ambulatory circuit around a contemplative space could be as effective in the lay as in the Christian realm. By its very nature, life inflicts on us universal pains based on time-less psychological and social realities; we all wrestle with the dilemmas of childhood, education, family, work, love, ageing and death – many of which now bear semi-official labels ('ado-lescent angst', 'postpartum depression', 'midlife crisis'). New secular cycles of representative sorrows could anchor them-selves around these stages and so articulate the true nature of their camouflaged dimensions. They could teach us lessons about the real course of life in the safety and quiet of a gallery, before events themselves found a way of doing the same with their characteristic violence and surprise.

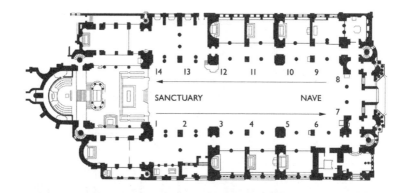

Station 9: Jesus Falls a Third Time, from Eric Gill's Fourteen Stations of the Cross, Westminster Cathedral, 1918.

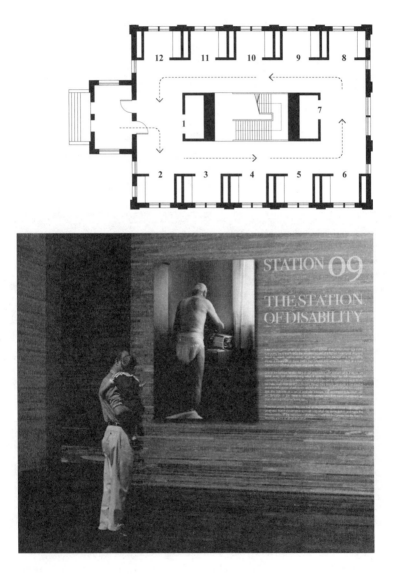

Station 9: The Station of Disability, from an imaginary secular
Twelve Stations of Old Age.

5.

Christian art understands that images are important partly because they can generate compassion, the fragile quality which enables the boundaries of our egos to dissolve, helps us to recognize ourselves in the experiences of strangers and can make their pain matter to us as much as our own.

Art has a role to play in this manoeuvre of the mind upon which, not coincidentally, civilization itself is founded, because the unsympathetic assessments we make of others are usually the result of nothing more sinister than our habit of looking at them in the wrong way, through lenses clouded by distraction, exhaustion and fear, which blind us to the fact that they are really, despite a thousand differences, just altered versions of ourselves: fellow fragile, uncertain, flawed beings likewise craving love and in urgent need of forgiveness.

As if to reinforce the idea that to be human is, above all else, to partake in a common vulnerability to misfortune, disease and violence, Christian art returns us relentlessly to the flesh, whether in the form of the infant Jesus's plump cheeks or of the taut, broken skin over his ribcage in his final hours. The message is clear: even if we do not bleed to death on a cross, simply by virtue of being human we will each of us suffer our share of agony and indignity, each face appalling, intractable realities which may nevertheless kindle in us feelings of mutuality. Christianity hints that if our bodies were immune to pain or decay, we would be monsters.

Michelangelo Buonarroti, *Pietà*, 1499.

A cancer patient after chemotherapy, by Preston Gannaway, 2008.

Picturing others as children can prompt similar moments of identification. It is no coincidence that, next to scenes of the Crucifixion, Jesus's babyhood is the most frequent theme in Christian art, his infant innocence and sweetness contrasting poignantly with the way we know his story will end. Images of Jesus sleeping in his mother's arms subliminally reinforce his counsel that we should learn to regard all our fellow human beings as if they were children. Our enemies too were once infants, in need of attention rather than bad, fifty centimetres long, breathing softly on their stomachs, smelling of milk and talcum powder.

Though our destructive powers increase with age, though we shed the ability to elicit others' sympathy even as we acquire a greater store of things to be pitied for, we always retain some of the artlessness and lack of guile with which we began. In recounting one man's journey from the manger to the cross, Christianity tells a quasi-universal story about the fate of innocence and gentleness in a turbulent world. We are most of us lambs in need of good shepherds and a merciful flock.

6.

The unreliability of our native imaginative powers magnifies our need for art. We depend on artists to orchestrate moments of compassion to excite our sympathies on a regular basis; to create artificial conditions under which we can experience, in relation to the figures we see in works of art, some of what we might one day feel towards flesh-and-blood people in our own lives.

Top: Francisco de Zurbarán, *The Bound Lamb*, *c.* 1635. *Above:* what separates compassion from indifference is the angle of vision: Helen Levitt, *New York 1940*.

The possibility of responding compassionately to others is crucially linked to our angle of vision. According to our perspective, we may see either a self-righteous husband lecturing his wife or two wounded and humiliated individuals equally unable properly to articulate their distress; a proud battalion of soldiers in a village street or a frightened girl hiding from invaders in a doorway; an old man walking home with a bag of groceries or a former gold medallist in free-style swimming transformed into a stooped, sallow figure unrecognizable even to himself.

Looking at a photograph by Helen Levitt of four boys in a New York street, we are likely to find ourselves longing to comfort the grim-faced, stoic young man in the corner, whose mother perhaps only half an hour ago did up the many buttons of his handsome coat, and whose distressed expression evokes a pure form of agony. But how very different the same scene would have looked from just a metre away and another viewpoint. To the boy at the far right, what appears to matter most is a chance to take a closer look at his friend's toy. He has already lost any interest in the overdressed crybaby by the wall, whom he and his classmates have just slapped hard for a bit of fun, on this day as on most others.

Similarly, a compassionate response to Mantegna's hilltop panorama depends on how we are guided to look at Calvary. The sunny early afternoon, with its wispy clouds floating across a pale blue horizon, might have seemed exceptionally pleasant and trouble-free to the soldier walking home with his pike resting on his shoulder, and looking forward to a supper of an

Andrea Mantegna, *Crucifixion*, 1459.

omelette or a chicken leg. Gazing at the valley before him, with its vineyards and rivers, he would hardly have registered the usual moans emanating from the low-lifes up on the crosses. For his fellow soldiers seated on the ground, meanwhile, the most pressing question on the day of the death of the son of God might have been who was going to win five denarii in the game they were playing on the face of a shield.

The range of possible perspectives in any scene – and the range, therefore, of responses available to the viewer – reveals the responsibilities which fall to the makers of images: to direct us to those who deserve but often do not win our sympathy, to stand as witnesses to all that it would be easier for us to turn away from. The gravity of the task explains the privileged place accorded in the Christian tradition to St Luke, the patron saint of artists, who, legend tells us, was the first to depict the Crucifixion, and who is frequently represented in Christian art with brushes and paints in hand, taking in what the Roman soldiers pretended not to see.

7.

While bitter debate must always surround the larger question of what makes a good artist, in the context of religion the criteria are narrower and more straightforward: a good artist by Christian standards is one who successfully animates the important moral and psychological truths which are in danger of losing their hold on us amid the distracted conditions of daily existence. Christian artists know that their technical talents – their command of light, composition and colour, their mastery

A reminder of what courage is actually like: Rembrandt van Rijn, *Christ in the Storm on the Sea of Galilee*, 1633.

of their materials and media – find their ultimate purpose in calling forth appropriate ethical responses from us, so that our eyes can train our hearts.

Militating against this mission are all manner of visual clichés. The real difficulty with the ideas which underlie compassion is not that they seem surprising or peculiar, but rather that they seem far too obvious: their very reasonableness and ubiquity strip them of their power. To cite a verbal parallel, we have heard a thousand times that we should love our neighbour, but the prescription loses any of its meaning when it is merely repeated by rote.

So too with art: the most dramatic scenes, painted without talent or imagination, generate only indifference and boredom. The task for artists is therefore to find new ways of prising open our eyes to tiresomely familiar yet critical ideas. The history of Christian art comprises waves of assaults on the great old truths by geniuses who tried to ensure that viewers would be astonished anew and provoked to inner amendment by the humility of the Virgin, the fidelity of Joseph, the courage of Jesus or the sadism of the Jewish authorities.

All such efforts ultimately have a twofold purpose, in accordance with the basic precepts of Christianity: to encourage a revulsion towards evil and to excite a love of goodness. In both cases, inferior art is problematic, not for strictly aesthetic reasons, but because it fails to promote appropriate emotion and action. It is no easy thing to keep making hell vivid: the attempt can easily yield just another vat of burning flesh, one more in a redundant series which, in its formulaic horror, ends

If we're not careful, even hell gets boring. We need talented artists to evoke the moral commitment we otherwise lose touch with. *Top*: Fra Angelico, *Last Judgement* (detail), 1435. *Above*: Abid Katib, *Shifa hospital, Gaza*, 2008.

up touching no one. It takes more than bloodthirstiness to revive our disgust at cruelty. We can grow bored of seeing yet another painting of the seventh circle of hell or another photograph of the killing fields of Gaza – until a skilful artist stops us in our tracks with an image that finally brings home to us what is truly at stake.

Just as evil must continually be made new to help us sense its power, so too must goodness. Accordingly, Christian artists have tirelessly striven to render virtue vivid, to pierce through our cynicism and world-weariness and to lay before us depictions of individuals whom we should all wish to be a little bit more like.

8.

Naturally, Christian art does not treat all of the themes that we should bear in mind for the health of our souls. There is no shortage of topics it ignores: the role of self-discipline, the need for playfulness, the importance of honouring the fragility of the natural world ... But completeness isn't the point. For our purposes, Christianity is more interested in defining an overarching mission for art: to depict virtues and vices and remind us of what is important though prone to be forgotten.

Intriguingly, Christianity never expected its artists to decide what their works would be about; it was left to theologians and doctors of divinity to formulate the important themes, which were only then passed on to painters and sculptors and turned into convincing aesthetic phenomena. The Church implicitly wondered why a mastery of the technical aspects of art – a

Christianity suggests that we might stick to certain key themes and allow artists to achieve greatness principally through their interpretations. *Top*: Jean-Honoré Fragonard, *The Rest during the Flight to Egypt*, 1750. *Above*: Titian, *The Flight into Egypt*, *c*. 1504.

talent for making a dab of paint look like an elbow, or a patch of stone like hair – should be thought to be compatible with the ability to work out the meaning of life. The religion did not, on top of everything else, expect that Titian could be a gifted philosopher. It may be that we are asking too much of our own secular artists, requiring them not only to impress our senses but also to be the originators of profound psychological and moral insights. Our artistic scene might benefit from greater collaborations between thinkers and makers of images, a marriage of the best ideas with their highest expressions.

Christianity was also wise in not insisting that the concepts behind works of art should change all the time. There have been few more harmful doctrines for art than the Romantic belief that greatness must involve constant originality at a thematic level. Christian artists were able amply to express their unique skills, but had to stick to a set roster of topics, from the Annunciation to the Deposition. Their individual inclinations were subsumed within an overarching brief which spared them the relentless Romantic pressure to be original.

To specify that images must focus on the same ideas is not to demand that they should all look identical. Just as Titian's and Fragonard's versions of the holy family's *Flight into Egypt* look entirely different, so too a putative 'Sorrows of Infidelity' depicted by a contemporary photographer like Jeff Wall would not need to look anything like the same theme as handled by his colleagues Philip-Lorca diCorcia or Alec Soth.

9.

Although we have up to this point considered modern secular art only incidentally, and through the prism of photography, the model wherein art serves as a mechanism for reminding us of important ideas extends comfortably beyond the representational realm to include abstract works.

Though it can sometimes be hard to say quite what abstract pieces are *about*, we can sense their broad themes well enough and, when it is a question of great works, we welcome them into our lives for the same reasons as figurative images: because they put us back in touch with themes we need to keep close to us but are in danger of losing sight of. We sense virtues like courage and strength emanating from the stern steel slabs of Richard Serra. There are ever-necessary evocations of calm in the formal geometries of paintings by Agnes Martin, while poems on the role of tension in a good life lurk within the wood and string sculptures of Barbara Hepworth.

Buddhism has been provocative in suggesting that our response to abstract creations could be enhanced if we were given specific suggestions as to what we should be thinking about while we contemplate them. When faced with the complex patterns of mandalas, for instance, we are encouraged to narrow down their range of possible meanings and focus on them as sensuous representations of the harmony of the cosmos described in Buddhist theology. The religion additionally gives us mantras to repeat as we look, most often 'Om mani padme hum' (translated from the Sanskrit as 'Generosity-ethics-patience-diligence-renunciation-wisdom'), which sets

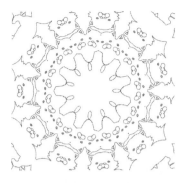

What separates the work of a contemporary abstract artist like Richard Long (*above*) from the tradition of the Buddhist mandala (*top*) is that Long's piece carries no liturgy, it does not tell us what we might think about as we look at it, and hence, regardless of its great formal beauty, it risks provoking reactions of bewilderment or tedium. Despite the powerful elite prejudice against guidance, works of art are not diminished by being accompanied by instruction manuals.

up a virtuous cycle whereby our eyes enrich our ideas while our ideas guide our vision.

Inspired by Buddhism's heavy-handed and yet productive curatorial directions, we might ask of many works of art that they tell us more explicitly what important notions they are trying sensually to remind us of, so as to rescue us from the hesitation and puzzlement that they may otherwise provoke. Despite a powerful elite prejudice against guidance, works of art are rarely diminished by being accompanied by instruction manuals.

10.

Aside from directing us to rethink the themes and purpose of art, religions also ask us to reconsider the categories under which works are arranged. Modern museums typically lead us into galleries arranged under headings such as 'The Nineteenth Century' and 'The Northern Italian School', which reflect the academic traditions in which their curators have been educated. However, this arrangement is no more responsive to the inner needs of museum-goers than is – to readers – the scholarly division of literature into such categories as 'The American Novel of the Nineteenth Century' or 'Carolingian Poetry'.

A more fertile indexing system would group together artworks from across genres and eras according to the concerns of our souls. Gallery tours would take us through spaces which would each try to remind us in a sensory way – with the help of unapologetic labels and catalogues – of important ideas related to a variety of problematic areas of our lives. There would be galleries devoted to evoking the beauty of simplicity (featuring works by Chardin and Choe Seok-Hwan), the curative powers of nature (Corot, Hobbema, Bierstadt, Yuan Jiang), the dignity of the outsider (Friedrich, Hopper, Starkey) or the comfort of maternal nurture (Hepworth, Cassatt). A walk through a museum would amount to a structured encounter with a few of the things which are easiest for us to forget and most essential and life-enhancing to remember.

In this revamping we might look for inspiration to the Venetian parish church of Santa Maria Gloriosa dei Frari. Proudly indifferent to the indexing methodology of the academic system, the Frari is committed to the mission of rebalancing our souls with a highly eclectic range of works, including a fresco by Paolo Veneziano (*c.* 1339), a statue of John the Baptist by Donatello (1438), Giovanni Bellini's *Madonna and Child with Saints* (1488) and a large altarpiece by Titian (1516–18). The building throws together sculptures, paintings, metalwork and window traceries from across centuries and regions because it is more interested in the coherence of art's impact on our souls than in the coherence of the origins and stylistic inclinations of the people who produced it.

By contrast, in terms of honouring the purpose of art, the apparent order of the modern museum is at heart a profound *dis*order. Scholastic traditions such as sorting works according to where or when they were created, grouping them by categories such as 'School of Venice' and 'School of Rome', or 'landscapes' and 'portraits', or separating them by genre – photography, sculpture, painting – prevent secular museums from achieving any real coherence at an emotional level, and therefore from laying claim to the true transformative power of the art arranged in churches and temples.

11.

The challenge is to rewrite the agendas for our museums so that art can begin to serve the needs of psychology as effectively as, for centuries, it has served those of theology. Curators should dare to reinvent their spaces so that they can be more than dead libraries for the creations of the past. These curators should co-opt works of art to the direct task of helping us to live: to achieve self-knowledge, to remember forgiveness and love and to stay sensitive to the pains suffered by our ever troubled species and its urgently imperilled planet. Museums must be more than places for displaying beautiful objects. They should be places that use beautiful objects in order to try to make us good and wise. Only then will museums be able to claim that they have properly fulfilled the noble but still elusive ambition of becoming our new churches.

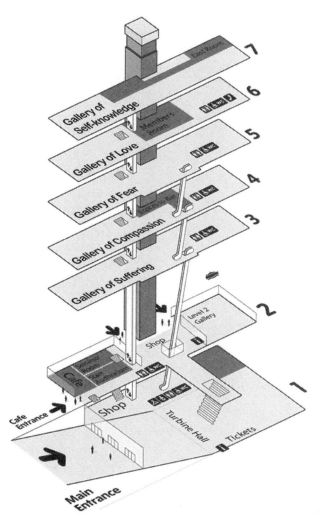

A new Tate Modern, London. If museums really were to be our new churches, the art wouldn't need to change, only the way it was arranged and presented. Each gallery would focus on bringing a set of important, rebalancing emotions to life.

IX

Architecture

1.

Given how ugly huge stretches of the modern world have become, one might wonder whether it really matters what things around us look like, whether the design of office towers, factories, depots and docks truly merits the consideration of anyone beyond those who directly own or use these structures. The implicit answer must be no. It is surely foolish, precious and ultimately dangerous to be overly receptive to whatever is in front of our eyes; otherwise, we would end up unhappy most of the time.

So far as the law is concerned, property development is just another branch of private enterprise. What counts is who owns a piece of land, not who is forced to stare at, and then suffer from, what has been built on it. The legal system is not geared to recognize the sensitivities of passers-by. To complain that a tower or motel offends the eye is not a category of distress that contemporary planners are skilful at honouring or addressing. In its tolerance of landscapes which generally leave us no option but to look at our feet, the modern world is resolutely, and in a secular sense, *Protestant*.

When Protestantism took hold in northern Europe in the first half of the sixteenth century, it manifested an extreme hostility towards the visual arts, attacking Catholics for their complicated and richly decorated buildings. 'For anyone to arrive at God the Creator, he needs only Scripture as his Guide and Teacher,' insisted John Calvin, giving voice to the anti-aesthetic sentiment of many in the new denomination. What mattered to Protestants was the written word. This, rather

Relief statues in the Cathedral of St Martin, Utrecht, attacked during campaigns of Reformation iconoclasm in the sixteenth century.

than elaborate architecture, would be enough to lead us to God. Devotion could be fostered by a Bible in a bare room just as well as it could in the nave of a jewel-encrusted cathedral. Indeed, there was a risk that through their sensory richness, sumptuous buildings could distract us, making us prefer beauty over holiness. It was no coincidence that Protestant reformers presided over repeated incidents of aesthetic desecration, during which statues were smashed, paintings burnt and alabaster angels brutally separated from their wings.

These same reformers meanwhile constrained their own architects to the design of sober and plain hangars which could shelter the members of a congregation from the rain while they read the Bible, but would leave them undistracted by any thoughts of the building they were in.

It was not long before Catholicism was goaded into a response. Following the Council of Trent in 1563, the papacy issued a decree insisting that, contrary to the impious suggestions of the Protestants, cathedrals, sculptures and paintings were in fact integral to the task of ensuring that 'the people could be instructed and confirmed in the habit of remembering, and continually revolving in mind the articles of faith'. Far from being a diversion, sacred architecture was a reminder of the sacramental truths: it was a devotional poem written in stone, wood and fragments of coloured glass. To drive home the argument, the Catholic Church inaugurated a massive programme of construction and decoration. Alongside the pale, featureless halls of the Reformation, there now arose a new generation of ecclesiastical buildings intended to breathe

Left: Chapel at Schloss Hartenfels, Torgau, Germany, 1544. *Right*: Chiesa del Gesù, Rome, 1584.

passionate emotion back into a threatened faith. Ceilings were overlaid with images of heaven, niches were crowded with saints and walls were affixed with heavy stucco mouldings, above frescoes depicting miraculous incidents in Jesus's ministry.

To derive a sense of the aesthetic gulf that had opened up between the two branches of Christianity, we need only compare the sobriety of the earliest extant Protestant chapel, at Schloss Hartenfels, in Torgau, Germany (1544), with the ecstasies of the nave vault ('the triumph of the name of Jesus') of Rome's Chiesa del Gesù (1584).

2.

In arguing for the importance of architecture, Catholicism was making a point, half touching, half alarming, about the way we function. It was suggesting that we suffer from a heightened sensitivity to what is around us, that we will notice and be affected by everything our eyes light upon, a vulnerability to which Protestantism has frequently preferred to remain blind or indifferent. Catholicism was making the remarkable allegation that we need to have good architecture around us in order to grow into, and remain, good people.

The foundations of Catholicism's respect for beauty can be traced back to the work of the Neoplatonic philosopher Plotinus, who in the third century AD made an explicit connection between beauty and goodness. For Plotinus, the quality of our surroundings counts because what is beautiful is far from being idly, immorally or self-indulgently 'attractive'. Beauty alludes to, and can remind us about, virtues like love, trust, intelligence, kindness and justice; it is a material version of goodness. If we study beautiful flowers, columns or chairs, Plotinus's philosophy proposed, we will detect in them properties that carry direct analogies with moral qualities and will serve to reinforce these in our hearts via our eyes.

Along the way, Plotinus's argument served to emphasize how seriously one would have to consider ugliness. Far from being merely unfortunate, ugliness was recategorized as a subset of evil. Ugly buildings were shown to contain equivalents of the very flaws that revolt us at an ethical level. No less than people, ugly buildings can be described using terms like brutal, cynical, self-satisfied or sentimental. Furthermore, we are no less vulnerable to their suggestions than we are to the behaviour of ill-intentioned acquaintances. Both give licence to our most sinister sides; both can subtly encourage us to be bad.

Not coincidentally, surely, it was the Protestant countries in Europe which first witnessed the extremes of ugliness that would become so typical of the modern world. Manchester, Leeds and other cities like them subjected their inhabitants to hitherto unparalleled degrees of unsightliness, as if they were testing to the full John Calvin's contention that architecture and art have no role to play in the condition of our souls and that a godly life can therefore satisfactorily unfold in a slum tenement with a view on to an open-cast coal mine, just so long as there is a Bible to hand.

This ideology did not pass unchallenged – and Catholicism once again had a hand in resisting it. When the nineteenth-century architect Augustus Pugin, a devout Catholic, considered the new landscapes of industrial England, he attacked them not merely for their appearance, but also for their power to destroy the human spirit. In two contrasting illustrations, he showed a typical English town, first as he imagined it had looked in the fifteenth century under an aesthetically sensitive Catholic regime and then, four centuries later, as it was in his own day, grossly blighted by the oppressive workhouses, mills and factories of the Protestant order. As Pugin saw it, Protestantism had directly promoted the reckless, hugely influential (and, for developers, hugely convenient) notion that one might destroy a city's appearance without in any way damaging the souls of its inhabitants.

It would be easy enough to accuse Pugin of gross partisanship and far-fetched aestheticism, but the more daunting and anxiety-producing possibility is that he was essentially right, if not in his attack on Protestants, then at least in his underlying assessment of the impact that visual forms can have on us. What if our minds are susceptible to more than just the books we read? What if we are also influenced by the houses, hospitals and factories around us? Might we not hence have good reason to mount protests against ugliness – and, despite a thousand obstacles, strive to put up buildings that could advance a case for goodness through their beauty?

3.

In the secular parts of the world, it is common, even among unbelievers, in fact especially among them, to lament the passing of the great days of religious architecture. It is common to hear

Might ugliness harm our souls? The Catholic city (*top*) versus the Protestant one (*above*) from Augustus Pugin, *Contrasts* (1836).

those who have no interest in the doctrines of religion admit to a nostalgia for ecclesiastical buildings: for the texture of stone walls on hillside chapels, for the profiles of spires glimpsed across darkening fields and perhaps for the sheer ambition involved in putting up a temple to house a book (Judaism) or a shrine to one of the rear molars of an enlightened saint (Theravada Buddhism). But these nostalgic musings are always cut short with a reluctant acknowledgement that an end to faith must inevitably mean an end to the possibility of temples.

Behind this assumption lies the implicit idea that where there are no more gods or deities, there can be nothing left to celebrate – and hence nothing more to emphasize through the medium of architecture.

Yet upon examination it in no way logically follows that an end to our belief in sacred beings must mean an end to our attachment to values or to our desire to provide a home for them through architecture. In the absence of gods, we still retain ethical beliefs which are in need of being solidified and celebrated. Any of those things which we revere but are inclined too often to overlook might justifiably merit the founding of its own 'temple'. There could be temples to spring and temples to kindness, temples to serenity and temples to reflection, temples to forgiveness and temples to self-knowledge.

What might a temple without a god in it look like? Throughout history, religions have been zealous in laying down uniform rules regarding the appearance of their buildings. For medieval Christians, all cathedrals were expected to have cruciform ground plans, east–west axes, water basins for baptisms at the western ends of naves and sanctuaries with altars at their eastern ends. To this day, South-East Asian Buddhists understand that their architectural energy has no option but to be channelled into constructing hemispherical stupas with parasols and circum-ambulatory terraces.

In the case of secular temples, however, there would be no need to follow such canonical laws. The temples' only common element would have to be their dedication to promoting virtues essential to the well-being of our souls. But which specific virtues would be honoured in the various venues, and how the idea of them would be successfully conveyed, could be entirely left up to their individual architects and patrons. The priority would be only to define a new typology of building rather than to design particular examples of it.

Nevertheless, to demonstrate the approach, we could outline a handful of possible themes for secular temples, along with a few architectural strategies to complement them.

– A Temple to Perspective

Considering how much of our lives we spend exaggerating our own importance and the magnitude of the insults and reversals which we suffer as a result, there could be few more pressing priorities for a new temple architecture than answering our need for perspective.

We seem unable to resist overstating every aspect of ourselves: how long we are on the planet for, how much it matters what we achieve, how rare and unfair are our professional failures, how rife with misunderstandings are our relationships, how deep are our sorrows. Melodrama is individually always the order of the day.

Religious architecture can perform a critical function in relation to this egoism (ultimately as painful as it is mistaken), because of its capacity to adjust our impressions of our physical – and as a consequence also our psychological – size, by playing with dimensions, materials, sounds and sources of illumination. In certain cathedrals that are vast in scale or hewn out of massive, antique-looking stones, or in others that are dark save for a single shaft of light filtering in from a distant oculus or silent but for the occasional sound of water dripping from a great height into a deep pool, we may feel that we are being introduced, with unusual and beguiling grace, to a not unpleasant sense of our own insignificance.

To be made to 'feel small' is, to be sure, a painful daily reality of the human playground. But to be made to feel small by something mighty, noble, accomplished and intelligent is to

The advantages of being made to feel small: Tadao Ando, Christian Church of the Light, Ibaraki, Japan, 1989.

have wisdom presented to us along with a measure of delight. There are churches that can induce us to surrender our egoism without in any way humiliating us. In them we can set aside our ordinary concerns and take on board (in a way we never dare to do when we are under direct fire from other humans) our own nullity and mediocrity. We can survey ourselves as if from a distance, no longer offended by the wounds inflicted on our self-esteem, feeling newly indifferent to our eventual fate, generous towards the universe and open-minded about its course.

Such feelings may visit us in non-ecclesiastical buildings too: in a massive, narrow tower with charred timber walls, in a concrete void extending five storeys underground or in a room lined with stones bearing the fossilized imprints of minuscule shelled ammonites which partook of life in the tropical waters of Laurentia (modern-day eastern North America and Greenland) during the Palaeozoic Age, some 300 million years before our first recognizable ancestor had the wit to stand upright or to fashion a canoe.

A new Temple to Perspective might end up playing with some of the same ideas as are explored in science museums and observatories. There might be items of palaeontological and geological interest in the walls, and astronomical instruments in the ceilings and roof. And yet there would be important distinctions between these two types of institution at the level of ambition. Like a science museum, a Temple to Perspective would hope to push us towards an awareness (always under threat in daily life) of the scale, age and complexity of the

A Temple to Perspective whose structure would represent the age of the earth, with each centimetre of height equating to 1 million years. Measuring 46 metres in all, the tower would feature, at its base, a tiny band of gold a mere millimetre thick, standing for mankind's time on earth.

universe, but unlike a science museum, it would not bother to pretend that the point of the exercise was to give us a grounding in a scientific education. It would not in the end matter very much whether visitors ever mastered the differences between, say, the Triassic and Cambrian eras, the detailed explanations of which are often so painfully laboured over by museum curators and yet so likely to have been forgotten by most of their audience by the time they reach the car park. This would be science roughly handled and presented in the interests of stirring awe rather than in the name of promoting knowledge, science leaned upon for its therapeutic, perspective-giving capacity rather than for its factual value.

– *A Temple to Reflection*

It is one of the unexpected disasters of the modern age that our new unparalleled access to information has come at the price of our capacity to concentrate on anything much. The deep, immersive thinking which produced many of civilization's most important achievements has come under unprecedented assault. We are almost never far from a machine that guarantees us a mesmerizing and libidinous escape from reality. The feelings and thoughts which we have omitted to experience while looking at our screens are left to find their revenge in involuntary twitches and our ever-decreasing ability to fall asleep when we should.

Because we are drawn in architecture to styles which seem to possess some of the qualities we lack in ourselves, it is little wonder that we should be readily seduced by spaces that are purified and free of distraction, and in which stimuli have been reduced to a minimum – places, perhaps, where the view has been carefully framed to take in a few rocks, or the branches of a tree, or a patch of sky, where the walls are solid, the materials are enduring and the only sound to be heard is that of wind or flowing water.

A Temple to Reflection would lend structure and legitimacy to moments of solitude. It would be a simple space, offering visitors little beyond a bench or two, a vista and a suggestion that they set to work on unravelling some of the troubling themes that they have been using their normal activity to suppress.

It is only in the age of the BlackBerry that large numbers of people can finally sense why monasteries were originally invented: Gougane Barra church, County Cork, Ireland, 1879.

A place to lay in wait for the shy, elusive insights: a Temple to Reflection.

There is a devilishly direct relationship between the significance of an idea and how nervous we become at the prospect of having to think about it. We can be sure that we have something especially crucial to address when the very notion of being alone grows unbearable. For this reason, religions have always been forceful in recommending that their followers observe periods of solitude, however much discomfort these might at first provoke. A modern Temple to Reflection would follow this philosophy, creating ideally reassuring conditions for contemplation, allowing us to wait in a restful bare room for those rare insights upon which the successful course of our life depends, but which normally run across our distracted minds only occasionally and skittishly like shy deer.

– *A Temple for the Genius Loci*

Among the more intriguing features of Imperial Roman religion was that it not only provided for the worship of cosmopolitan gods such as Juno and Mars (whose temples could be found all across the empire, from Hadrian's Wall to the banks of the Euphrates) but also allowed for the reverence of a panoply of local deities, whose personalities reflected the character, either topographical or cultural, of their native regions. These protective spirits, known as 'genii locorum', were given temples of their own and developed reputations – which sometimes drew travellers to them from afar – for being able to cure a variety of ailments of the mind and body. The spirits from the coastline south of Naples, for example, were thought to be particularly well suited to the abatement of melancholy, while the genius loci of Colonia Iulia Equestris (modern-day Nyon, on the shore of Lake Geneva) was supposed to have a special talent for consoling those oppressed by the vagaries of political and commercial life.

Like so much else that seems sensible about Roman religion, the tradition of the genius loci was absorbed by Christianity, which made comparable connections between specific localities and their curative powers, though it chose to talk of shrines rather than temples, and of saints instead of spirits. The map of medieval Europe was dotted with holy sites, many of them built upon Roman foundations, which promised to grant the faithful relief from their physical and mental ills via contact with assorted body parts of dead Christian saints.

A Pilgrimage Map of Medieval Europe

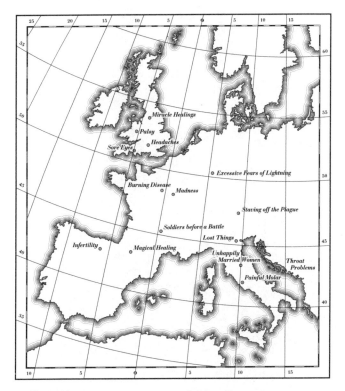

⊙ *Altötting, Germany*
Staving off the Plague (Virgin Mary)

⊙ *Bad Münstereifel, Germany*
Excessive Fears of Lightning (St Donatus)

⊙ *Barrios de Colina, Spain*
Infertility (San Juan de Ortega)

⊙ *Buxton, England*
Miracle Healings (St Anne)

⊙ *Chartres, France*
Burning Disease (St Anthony)

⊙ *Conques, France*
Soldiers before a Battle (St Foy)

⊙ *Dubrovnik, Croatia*
Throat Problems (St Blaise)

⊙ *Hereford, England*
Palsy (St Ethelbert)

⊙ *Larchant, France*
Madness (St Mathurin)

⊙ *Lourdes, France*
Magical Healing (St Bernadette)

⊙ *Morcombelake, England*
Sore Eyes (St Wite)

⊙ *Padua, Italy*
Lost Things (St Anthony of Padua)

⊙ *Rome, Italy; Basilica of San Lorenzo*
Painful Molar (St Apollonia)

⊙ *Spoleto, Italy*
Unhappily Married Women
(St Rita of Cascia)

⊙ *Windsor Castle (Royal Chapel), England*
Headaches ('Good King Henry [VI]')

The underlying spiritual seriousness of the souvenir industry: a fourteenth-century badge from the shrine of Thomas Becket, in Canterbury.

Believers with painful dental issues, for instance, knew to travel to the Basilica of San Lorenzo in Rome, where they could touch the arm bones of St Apollonia, the patron saint of teeth. Unhappily married women went to Umbria to visit the shrine of St Rita of Cascia, patron saint of marital problems. Soldiers looking to embolden themselves before battle might commune with the bones of St Foy, kept in a gold-plated reliquary in the abbey-church of Conques, in southwestern France. Women who were having difficulty breast-feeding could find comfort at the Shrine of the Holy Breast Milk in Chartres. And those with excessive lightning phobias were commended to the German town of Bad Münstereifel, where they could lay their hands on the relics of St Donatus, renowned for relieving fears of fire and explosions.

On their arrival at the appropriate shrine, pilgrims would first head for the nearby shops that sold moulded wax models of the troublesome parts of themselves, from legs, ears and breasts to penises and even whole souls (in the form of babies). Once inside the shrines themselves, they would place their effigies on altars, tombs or caskets, kneel in prayer and beg the spirits of the saints for their help.

Afterwards, the pilgrims would repair to souvenir stalls. Following the declaration by the fourth-century theologian Cyril of Jerusalem that handkerchiefs which came into contact with the bodies of the martyrs would forever possess a supernatural power, these stalls had begun to carry plentiful supplies of linens. They also offered small glass vials containing dust from the floors around the saints' tombs, which could be resorted to for assistance in moments of distress. A Benedictine monk named Guibert of Nogent once reported that a friend who had accidentally swallowed a toad and nearly choked to death was saved by a teaspoonful of dust from the tomb of St Marcel, Bishop of Paris. Most commonly, visitors were invited to acquire finely sculpted lead badges showing the face of the saint whose relics they had come to see. It was said of Louis XI of France, who had stopped in at every notable shrine in his country, that his hat was 'brim-full of images which he kissed whenever good or bad news arrived'.

Although few of us would today walk a hundred kilometres to seek help for a fear of lightning, travelling nevertheless remains at the heart of many secular ideas of fulfilment. Our trips retain a role in cementing important inner transitions. While we might call them valuable rather than holy, there are places which by virtue of their remoteness, solitude, beauty or cultural richness retain an ability to salve the wounded parts of us.

Unfortunately, we lack any reliable mechanism or method for identifying these rare and curative locations. Here again, as so often when it comes to our emotional needs in the secular world, we miss the structure once provided for us by religions. Travel agents see themselves as being responsible solely for handling logistical matters – booking connecting flights, negotiating discounts on plane tickets and hotel rooms – and make little effort to help customers find their way to destinations that might bring a targeted benefit to their inner selves. We need psychoanalytically astute travel agents who could carefully analyse our deficiencies and match us up with parts of the world which would have the power to heal us – agents who would send us on travels to connect up with those qualities which we esteem but cannot generate in sufficient quantities at home.

We further suffer from a lack of shrines. Having arrived at our destination, we seldom know what to do with ourselves. We wander around in search of a centre. We long for a plausible crucible of significance, for somewhere, *anywhere* to go in order that we may touch the essence of the genius loci, but in the absence of alternatives we usually end up listlessly touring a museum, ashamed of ourselves for the strength of our desire to go back to our hotel and lie down.

How much more therapeutic our journeys might be if they could include a visit to a secular local shrine or temple, a work of architecture that would define and concentrate the qualities of its surrounding setting. Inside, we could deposit wax versions of our anxieties and immaturities, attempting thereby to formalize the purpose of our trip – while outside, in a row of small retail spaces, talented artists would sell inspiring tokens of the transformative powers of their settings.

One such shrine might be dedicated to the energy of a capital city, another to the purifying calmness of the deserted tundra, a third to the promises of the tropical sun. These temples would offer homes to otherwise elusive genii locorum, and together teach us to regard travel as a means of existential healing, rather than merely a source of entertainment or relaxation.

A psychotherapeutic travel agency would align mental disorders with the parts of the planet best able to alleviate them.

4.

There is no need to catalogue here all the themes that a new generation of temples might take up. There is in the end room in the world for as many different kinds of temple as there are varieties of need.

The point is only to argue that we should revive and continue the underlying aims of religious architecture, by expressing these through secular temples designed to promote important emotions and abstract themes, rather than through sacred shrines dedicated to embodied deities.

No less than the church spires in the skyscapes of medieval Christian towns, these temples would function as reminders of our hopes. They would vary in terms of their style, dimensions and forms – they could range from huts to hangars, they could be made of recycled tyres or gold tiles, they could hang from the sides of office buildings or be buried in illuminated grottoes under the streets – but they would all be connected through the ancient aspiration of sacred architecture: to place us for a time in a thoughtfully structured three-dimensional space, in order to educate and rebalance our souls.

X

Institutions

i. Books vs. Institutions

1.

When sceptics and atheists began their assaults on religion in the late eighteenth century, they did so primarily through the medium of books. They wondered in print whether a dead man could really roll back a tombstone and make his way unaided into the upper atmosphere, whether a young woman could be immaculately impregnated by a deity, whether battles could be won by the intercession of angels or earaches cured by contact with the shin bone of a martyred saint (Cornelius). And they tended to conclude their arguments by looking forward to the day when mankind might replace its superstitions with rationally based ideas, of the sort they admired in works of secular science, philosophy, literature and poetry.

Although these sceptics proved to be caustically entertaining critics of the faiths, they failed to appreciate the fundamental difference between themselves and their enemies: the latter were not relying primarily on the publication of *books* to achieve their impact. They were employing *institutions*, marshalling enormous agglomerations of people to act in concert upon the world through works of art, buildings, schools, uniforms, logos, rituals, monuments and calendars.

While laying out ideas in books which might sell anywhere from a few hundred copies to a few hundred thousand at very best may seem a noble enough ambition, the medium itself claims a dispiritingly meagre reach compared to the wide-ranging influence which institutions can wield in the development and perpetuation of attitudes and behaviours. In his *Republic*, Plato conveyed a touching understanding (born from experience) of the limits of the lone intellectual, when he remarked that the world would not be set right until philosophers became kings, or kings philosophers. In other words, writing books can't be enough if one wishes to change things. Thinkers must learn to master the power of institutions for their ideas to have any chance of achieving a pervasive influence on the world.

However, secular intellectuals have, unfortunately, long suffered from a temperamental suspicion of institutions, rooted in the Romantic worldview which has coloured cultural life since the nineteenth century. Romanticism has taught us to mock the ponderousness and strictures of institutions, their tendencies to corruption and their tolerance of mediocrity. The ideal of the intellectual has been that of a free spirit living beyond the confines of any system, disdainful of money, cut off from practical affairs and privately proud of being unable to read a balance sheet.

If people's inner lives remain even today more likely to be influenced by the biblical prophets than by secular thinkers, it is due in large part to the fact that the latter have been consistently unwilling to create institutional structures through which their soul-related ideas might be successfully disseminated to a wider audience. Those with an interest in addressing the needs of the secular soul have typically lacked scale, stable conditions of employment and the capacity to transmit their views through the mass media. Instead, volatile individual practitioners run what are in effect cottage industries, while organized religions infiltrate our consciousness with all the might and sophistication available to institutional power.

The modern world is not, of course, devoid of institutions. It is filled with commercial corporations of unparalleled size which have an intriguing number of organizational traits in common with religions. But these corporations focus only on our outer, physical needs, on selling us cars and shoes, pizzas and telephones. Religion's great distinction is that while it has a collective power comparable to that of modern corporations pushing the sale of soap and mashed potatoes, it addresses precisely those inner needs which the secular world leaves to disorganized and vulnerable individuals.

The challenge is hence to create – via a study of religious institutions – secular entities that could meet the needs of the inner self with all the force and skill that corporations currently apply to satisfying the needs of the outer.

2.
Among the fundamental lessons of religions as institutions are the importance of scale and the benefits that flow from being able properly to aggregate money, intelligence and status.

Whereas Romanticism glorifies the achievements of singular heroes, religions know how much will be impossible if individuals act alone. Outside of an organization, we may now and then succeed in securing a brief spike of fame for ourselves, but we will never be able to place our achievements on a stable footing, consistently replicate our insights or bridge our weaknesses. Sole authorship cannot be a logical long-term response to solving the

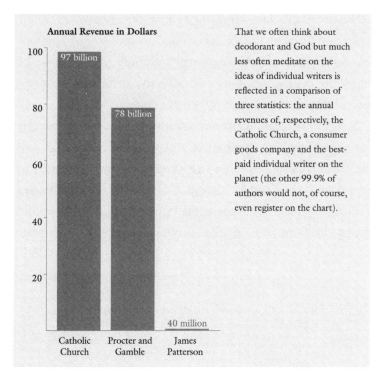

Annual Revenue in Dollars

97 billion

78 billion

40 million

Catholic Church

Procter and Gamble

James Patterson

That we often think about deodorant and God but much less often meditate on the ideas of individual writers is reflected in a comparison of three statistics: the annual revenues of, respectively, the Catholic Church, a consumer goods company and the best-paid individual writer on the planet (the other 99.9% of authors would not, of course, even register on the chart).

complexities of significant issues. We should ask why in matters of the soul we continue to believe in cloistered, companionless methods of assembly that we long ago disavowed in relation to the manufacture of pharmaceuticals or aircraft.

Then there is the matter of income. Institutions spare their members the humiliations and terrors of the sole trader. Their ability to pool capital, distribute it between projects and let it accumulate over decades enables them to survive lean periods and make adequate investments in research, marketing, recruitment and technology.

Whatever modern democracies may tell themselves about their commitment to free speech and to diversity of opinion, the values of a given society will uncannily match those of whichever organizations have the scale to pay for runs of thirty-second slots around the nightly news bulletin.

Scale has a similar impact on recruitment. Wealthy institutions can attract the best members of a generation, rather than just the blindly devoted or the irrationally committed. They can appeal to the large and psychologically healthy pool of candidates who care as much about garnering esteem and material comfort as they do about bettering the lot of mankind.

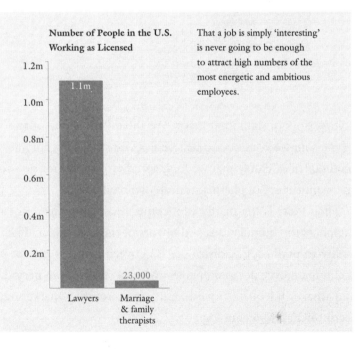

Number of People in the U.S. Working as Licensed

That a job is simply 'interesting' is never going to be enough to attract high numbers of the most energetic and ambitious employees.

Consider the respective careers of Thomas Aquinas and Friedrich Nietzsche. Some of the differences between their fates came down to the relative mental stability of the two men, but a good share of Aquinas's equanimity must also be attributed to the benevolent spiritual and material atmosphere he benefited from, first at the University of Paris, where he was Regent Master, and then at the theological college he helped to found in Naples. Nietzsche felt he lived by contrast (and in his own words) 'like a wild animal hunted out of every lair'. His life's project – to replace Christian morality with a secular ideology revolving around philosophy, music and art – found no favour with nineteenth-century German academia, forcing the philosopher into nomadic exile. Although he is frequently celebrated as a supreme exemplar of heroic individualism, the philosopher would in truth have appreciated nothing more than to exchange his isolation for a collegial establishment which could have lent his ideas a greater weight in the world.

Institutions have the added benefit of being able to offer permanent status to individuals simply on the basis of their membership, saving them from having to earn it on their own, over and over again, year by year. A lone thinker may be near the end of his or her life – or even, like Nietzsche, long dead – before the public notices that a good idea has sprung from someone without corporate status. Within an institution, all members can tap into a reputation built up by illustrious forebears and reinforced by elegant buildings and sleek bureaucratic processes. They can take on an ancient title – priest or archdeacon, professor or minister – and make use, for genuine ends, of the resources and lustre stored within a structure that is larger and more enduring than themselves.

Many would no doubt argue that modern society must already have all the institutions it needs. In practice, however, those who are drawn to what Catholicism has termed *cura animarum*, 'the care of souls', but who feel unable to effect this care in religious ways, are all too likely to end up compromised for want of a coherent network of colleagues, a tolerable income and a stable and dignified professional structure within which to operate. It is a measure of how deeply ingrained the problem is that we would even now struggle to give Nietzsche a professional home.

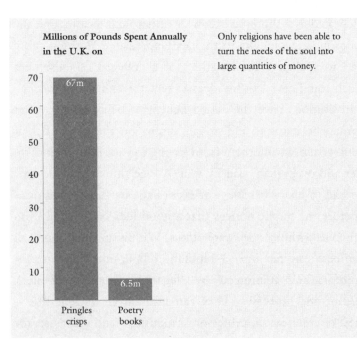

Millions of Pounds Spent Annually in the U.K. on

Only religions have been able to turn the needs of the soul into large quantities of money.

3.

Another useful feature of institutions is their ability to coalesce the efforts of their members through a shared visual vocabulary. Here again, the strategies of religions and commercial corporations overlap. While the sight of a cross emblazoned on the side of an ecclesiastical building or a lamb embroidered on an altar cloth has frequently prompted the observation that Christianity was an early and adept practitioner of the same kind of 'branding' that our modern corporations specialize in, the truth is, of course, the reverse: it is the corporations that have faithfully adopted the lessons in identity pioneered by religions.

The most important function of a brand is to promote consistency. Institutions trust that the appearance of their logo, whether on a remote mountainside or on top of a skyscraper, on a bedsheet or on a cloak, will instantly communicate the reliable presence of a particular set of values and act as a promise of uniformity and quality.

The enemy of branding is local variation. Here too we sense a certain tension between Romantic and institutional values, for whereas Romanticism appreciates the charms of the particular and the regional, the home-made and the spontaneous, institutions cannot forget the hazards of provincial initiatives. Instead of touching improvements on the rules of the centre, they see only depressing deviations from minimal standards. They are reminded of corruption, laziness, degeneracy and the abandonment of initial ambitions. To stamp out eccentricities, the training manual for new staff of the McDonald's Corporation runs to 300 pages, providing

instructions for every imaginable action and transaction: there are rules about where the employee's name badge must be placed, what sort of smile each customer must be treated to and precisely how much mayonnaise should be added to the underside of every top bun. The hamburger company has little faith in what the members of its workforce will do if left to their own devices.

In this, at least, McDonald's has much in common with the Catholic Church, which has similarly spent a good deal of its history struggling to ensure a regularity of service across a vast and scattered labour force. Taken collectively, its edicts – specifying details down to what sort of wine should be used at Holy Communion and what colour priests' shoes ought to be – indicate extreme concern about the standards of its peripheral branches. Following the Fourth Council of the Lateran, convoked by Pope Innocent III in 1213, the Church decreed (with evident irritation over the frequency with which even such basic rules were being broken) that 'clerics shall not attend the performance of mimes, entertainers or actors. They shall not visit taverns except in case of necessity, namely when on a journey. They are forbidden to play dice or games of chance or be present at them.' And lest some be tempted to show flair in their hairstyles, it was added that 'they must always have a shaved crown and tonsure'.

Heavy-handed though such decrees may have been, they helped to establish and enforce the consistent standards of ritual and performance that the faithful came to expect from the Church, and that all of us have in turn come to expect from corporations.

The advantages of an institutional delivery of soul-related needs: Father Chris Vipers listens to a confession at St Lawrence's Church, Feltham, England, 2010.

It is a singularly regrettable feature of the modern world that while some of the most trivial of our requirements (for shampoo and moisturizers, for example, as well as pasta sauce and sunglasses) are met by superlatively managed brands, our essential needs are left in the disorganized and unpredictable care of lone actors. For a telling illustration of the practical effects of branding and the quality control it is typically accompanied by, we need only compare the fragmented, highly variable field of psychotherapy with the elegantly discharged ritual of confession within the Catholic faith. Confession, well regimented in its every particular since the latter part of the fourteenth century, thanks to a stream of papal edicts and Vatican-issued manuals, is an epitome of the sort of reliable global service industry that would become the norm for consumer goods only in the mid-twentieth century. Everything from the positioning of the confessional box to the tone of voice used by the priest is governed by explicit rules, designed to assure all Catholics from Melbourne to Anchorage that their expectations for a redemptive examination of their soul will be met. No such provisions apply to our closest secular equivalent. Psychotherapy as currently practised lacks any consistency of setting or even any benchmarks for such apparently small yet critical details as the wording of the message on the therapist's answering machine, his or her dress code and the appearance of the consulting room. Patients are left to endure a run of local quirks, from encounters with their therapists' pets or children to gurgling pipework and bric-a-brac furnishings.

An imaginary branded chain of psychotherapists. Why should only phones and shampoos benefit from coherent retail identities?

4.

After successfully defining their identity, many corporations have gone on to engage in what business writers refer to as 'brand extension', the process whereby a company revered for its approach in one commercial sector carries over its values into another. Companies that began by making suits, for example, have realized that their values could just as effectively be applied to the design of belts and sunglasses, from which point it was only a short leap to imagine translation into furniture, then restaurants, apartments and eventually whole holiday resorts. These companies have wisely recognized that their customers' allegiance is to an ethos rather than to a single product, and that the beauty and goodness that were first distinguished in a tie could be no less present in a chair leg, an entrée or a sun lounger.

Inertia or unnecessary modesty has to date, however, prevented the most vigorous of modern companies from extending their brands across the full range of human requirements and, most cogently for the purposes of the present discussion, from applying their expertise to the apex of Maslow's famous pyramid of needs. Corporations have instead chosen to set up shop along the base of this pyramid, making minor improvements to services and products designed to help us to sleep, eat, be safe or move while leaving unaddressed our desire to self-actualize, learn, love and inwardly grow. It is a failing of historic proportions, for instance, that BMW's concern for rigour and precision has ended so conclusively at the bumpers of its cars rather than stretching to the founding of a school or of a political party, or that Giorgio Armani's eponymous corporation has determinedly skirted the possibility of running a therapy unit or a liberal arts college.

Intellectual movements have likewise, and just as regrettably, shunned attempts at brand extension. They have failed to imagine that their ideas could generate complementary, analogous services and products in the material realm, and become more vivid to us for having physical equivalents.

What makes religions so distinctive is that they have dared to assert coherent brand identities across a diverse range of areas, from the strictly intellectual and theological to the aesthetic, sartorial and culinary. Christianity, Judaism and Buddhism have all succeeded in relating larger ideas about the salvation of mankind to such subordinate material activities as managing weekend retreats, radio stations, restaurants, museums, lecture halls and clothing lines.

Because we are embodied creatures – sensory animals as well as rational beings – we stand to be lastingly influenced by concepts only when they come at us through a variety of channels. As religions seem alone in properly understanding, we cannot be adequately marked by ideas unless, in addition to being delivered through books, lectures and newspapers, they are also echoed in what we wear, eat, sing, decorate our houses with and bathe in.

Brand extension: Mr Giorgio Armani and Mr Mohamed Alabbar, Chairman of Emaar Properties, at the opening of the Armani Hotel Dubai, March 2010.

5.

One way of describing the activities of companies and religions is as forms of commodification – the process whereby haphazardly available, ill-defined goods are transformed into named, recognizable, well-stocked and well-presented entities.

We are familiar enough with this process as it is carried out by corporations trading in material things: time and again, companies have scoured the globe in search of previously scarce consumer items and brought regularity to the supply of tea and paprika, kiwis and papaya, sparkling water and jojoba oil. Religions have demonstrated comparable abilities in the spiritual realm, managing, through the use of ritual, to rescue moments and feelings that under other circumstances might have been overlooked or forgotten, but which have instead – thanks to a religious version of commodification – acquired ennobling names and fixed dates in calendars.

We have almost all had the experience of gazing at the night sky in September, when the alignment of the planets makes the full moon look especially bright and close by. We may briefly have pondered its majesty and the challenge it poses to our normal, earth-centric perspective. But those of us who are neither astronomers nor astronauts are unlikely to have formalized our lunar observation in any way, or indeed to have given it much further thought beyond a few minutes of contemplation.

For Zen Buddhists in Japan, however, the ritual known as *tsukimi* has thoroughly commodified the business of moon-watching. Every year, on the fifteenth day of the eighth month

Fixing appointments to appreciate the moon: a viewing platform used for *tsukimi* celebrations, Katsura Imperial Villa, Kyoto.

of the traditional Japanese lunisolar calendar, followers gather at nightfall around specially constructed cone-shaped viewing platforms, where for several hours prayers are read aloud which use the moon as a springboard for reflections on Zen ideas of impermanence. Candles are lit and white rice dumplings called *tsukimi dango* are prepared and shared out among strangers in an atmosphere at once companionable and serene. A feeling is thereby supported by a ceremony, by architecture, by good company and by food – and so lent a secure place in every Japanese Zen Buddhist's life.

Religions bring scale, consistency and outer-directed force to what might otherwise always remain small, random, private moments. They give substance to our inner dimensions – precisely those parts of us which Romanticism prefers to leave unregulated, for fear of hampering our chances of authenticity. They don't solely relegate our feelings to volumes of poetry or essays, knowing that books are in the end hushed objects in a noisy world. When it is springtime, Judaism takes hold of us with a force that Wordsworth or Keats never employed: at the first blossoming of trees, the faithful are told to gather outdoors with a rabbi and together recite the *birkat ilanot*, a ritual prayer from the Talmud honouring the hand that made the blossom:

> Blessed are you, Lord our God, King of the Universe,
> Who did not leave a single thing lacking in His world,
> Filling it with the finest creatures and trees,
> So as to give pleasure to all of mankind.
>
> (Talmud, Berakhot, 33:2)

Though the modern world encourages us to feel things spontaneously and at our own pace, religions are wiser in putting dates in our diaries: here, the Jewish festival of Birkat Ilanot.

We need institutions to foster and protect those emotions to which we are sincerely inclined but which, without a supporting structure and a system of active reminders, we will be too distracted and undisciplined to make time for.

The secular, Romantic world sees in commodification only loss, of diversity, quality and spontaneity. But at its finest the process enables fragile, rare but important aspects of existence to be more easily identified and more dependably shared. Those of us who hold no religious or supernatural beliefs still require regular, ritualized encounters with concepts such as friendship, community, gratitude and transcendence. We cannot rely on being able to make our way to them on our own. We need institutions that can remind us that we need them and present them to us in appealing wrappings – thus ensuring the nourishment of the most forgetful and un-self-aware sides of our souls.

6.

Plato's hope that philosophers might be kings, and kings philosophers, was to be partially realized many hundreds of years after he expressed it in the *Republic*, when in AD 313, thanks to the efforts of Emperor Constantine, Jesus took up his position at the head of a gigantic state-sponsored Christian Church and thereby became the first quasi-philosophical ruler to succeed in propagating his beliefs with institutional support. A similar combination of power and thought can be found in all the major religions, alliances which we can admire and learn from without necessarily subscribing to any of their ideologies.

The question we face now is how to ally the very many good ideas which currently slumber in the recesses of intellectual life with those organizational tools, many of them religious in origin, which stand the best chance of giving them due impact in the world.

ii: Auguste Comte

1.

This book is not the first to attempt to reconcile an antipathy towards the supernatural side of religion with an admiration for certain of its ideas and practices; nor is it the first to be interested in a practical rather than a merely theoretical effect. Out of the many efforts in this line, the most determined was undertaken in the nineteenth century by the visionary, eccentric and only intermittently sane French sociologist Auguste Comte.

Comte's ideas proceeded from a characteristically blunt observation that in the modern world, thanks to the discoveries of science, it would no longer be possible for anyone intelligent to believe in God. Faith would henceforth be limited to the uneducated, the fanatical, children and those suffering the final stages of incurable diseases. At the same time, Comte recognized, as many of his contemporaries did not, that a secular society devoted solely to the accumulation of wealth, scientific discovery, popular entertainment and romantic love – a society lacking in any sources of ethical instruction, consolation, transcendent awe or solidarity – would fall prey to untenable social maladies.

Comte's solution was neither to cling blindly to sacred traditions nor to cast them collectively and belligerently aside, but rather to identify their more relevant and rational aspects and put them to use. The resulting programme, the outcome of decades' worth of thought and the summit of Comte's intellectual achievement, was a new religion, a religion for atheists or, as Comte termed it, a Religion of Humanity, an original creed expressly tailored to the specific emotional and intellectual demands of modern man, rather than to the needs of the inhabitants of Judaea at the dawn of the Christian era or of northern India four centuries before that.

Comte presented his new religion in two volumes, the *Summary Exposition of the Universal Religion* and the *Theory of the Future of Man*. He was convinced that humanity was still at the beginning of its history and that all kinds of innovation – however bold and far-fetched they might initially sound – were possible in the religious field, just as in the scientific one. There was no need to stay loyal to beliefs dating from a time when humans had barely learned how to fashion a wheel, let alone build a steam engine. As Comte pointed out, no one intent on starting a new religion from scratch in the modern era would dream of proposing anything as hoary and improbable as the rituals and precepts bequeathed to us by our ancestors. The age he lived in, he asserted, afforded him a historic opportunity to edit out the absurdities of the past and to create a new version of religion which could be embraced because it was appealing and useful, rather than be clung to because it induced fear and represented itself as the only passport to a better life.

Comte was a keen historian of the faiths and his new religion turned out to be made up largely from some of the best bits of the old ones. He drew most heavily from Catholicism, which he judged to be abhorrent in the majority of its beliefs yet nonetheless well stocked with valuable insights about morality,

Rather than complain about the shortcomings of existing religions, it may sometimes be better just to invent a new one: Auguste Comte, 1798–1857.

art and ritual – and also essayed occasional forays into the theology of Judaism, Buddhism and Islam.

Comte sought above all else to correct the dangers to which he felt modern atheists were exposed. He believed that capitalism had aggravated people's competitive, individualistic impulses and distanced them from their communities, their traditions and their sympathies with nature. He criticized the nascent mass media for coarsening sensibilities and closing off chances for self-reflection, seclusion and original thought. In the same breath, he blamed the cult of Romanticism for putting too much strain on the conventional family and for promoting a falsely egoistic understanding of love. He lamented the arbitrary way in which, as soon as people felt they could no longer credit Jesus's status as a divine being, they also had to forgo all the wisdom promulgated by Christianity. Comte at first hoped that secular schools and universities could become the new educators of the soul, imparting ethical lessons rather than mere information to their students, but he came to realize that capitalism would in the end always favour a skilled, obedient and unintrospective workforce over an inquisitive and emotionally balanced one.

Comte's overall scheme for his religion began with a plan for an enormous new priesthood, which would employ 100,000 people in France alone. Despite the shared title, these priests were to be very different from those of the Catholic Church: they would be married, well integrated into the community and entirely secular, combining the skills of philosophers, writers and what we would now call psychotherapists. Their mission was to nurture the capacities for happiness and the moral sense of their fellow citizens. They would engage in therapeutic conversations with those plagued by problems at work or in love, deliver secular sermons and write jargon-free philosophical texts on the art of living. Along the way, this new priesthood would provide steady employment for the sort of people (among whose ranks Comte counted himself) who possessed a strong desire to help others and cultural and aesthetic interests, but who had been stymied by an inability to find work in universities and were thus forced to eke out an insecure living by writing for newspapers or peddling books to an indifferent public.

Because Comte appreciated the role that architecture had once played in bolstering the claims of the faiths, he proposed the construction of a network of secular churches – or, as he called them, churches for humanity. These would be paid for by bankers, for in his estimation the emergent banking class contained an unusually high proportion of individuals who were not only extremely wealthy but also intelligent, interested in ideas and capable of being swayed towards goodness. In a gesture of gratitude, the exterior façades of these secular churches would feature prominent busts of their banker-donors, while inside large halls would be decorated with portraits of the pantheon of the new religion's secular saints, including Cicero, Pericles, Shakespeare and Goethe, all singled out by the founder for their capacity to inspire and reassure us. Above a west-facing stage, inscribed in large gold letters, an aphorism would sum up Comte's belief in intellectual self-help:

'*Connais-toi pour t'ameliorer*' ('Know yourself to improve yourself'). Priests would deliver daily talks on such subjects as the importance of being kind to one's spouse, patient with one's colleagues, earnest in one's work and compassionate towards the less fortunate. Churches would become the locus for a continuous round of festivals of Comte's own inventive design: in the springtime there would be a celebration in honour of wives and mothers, in the summer, one to mark the momentous contribution of the iron industry to human progress and in the winter a third to offer thanks to domestic and farm animals like dogs, pigs and chickens.

Comte knew that the traditional faiths had cemented their authority by providing their adherents with daily or even hourly schedules of whom or what they ought to think about, rotas which were typically pegged to the commemoration of a holy figure or supernatural incident. So in the religion of humanity, every month would be officially devoted to a specific field of endeavour – from marriage and parenthood to art, science, agriculture and carpentry – and every day within that month to an individual who had made a significant contribution to a field. In November, the month of craft, the 12th, for example, would be the day of Richard Arkwright, the inventor of the industrial cotton-spinning mill, and the 22nd of Bernard Palissy, the Renaissance French potter, a model of endurance who famously tried for sixteen fruitless years to reproduce the glaze on Chinese porcelain.

2.

Regrettably, Comte's unusual, complex, sometimes deranged but always thought-provoking project was derailed by a host of practical obstacles. Its author was denounced by both atheists and believers, ignored by the general public and mocked by the newspapers. Towards the end of his life, despairing and frail, he took to writing long and somewhat threatening letters in defence of his religion to monarchs and industrialists across Europe – including Louis Napoleon, Queen Victoria, the Crown Prince of Denmark, the Emperor of Austria, 300 bankers and the head of the Paris sewage system – few of whom even bothered to reply, much less offered their financial support. Without seeing any of his ideas realized, Comte died at the age of fifty-nine, on 5 September 1857, or, according to his own calendar, in the month of philosophy, on the day honouring the achievements of the French astronomer Nicolas Lacaille, who in the eighteenth century had identified more than 10,000 stars in the southern hemisphere and now has a crater named after him on the dark side of the moon.

3.

Notwithstanding its many oddities, Comte's religion is hard to dismiss out of hand, for it identified important fields in atheistic society that continue to lie fallow and to invite cultivation and showed a pioneering interest in generating institutional support for ideas. His ability to sympathize with the ambitions of traditional religions, to study their methods and to adapt them to the needs of the modern world reflected a level of creativity, tolerance and inventiveness to which few later critics of religion have been capable of rising.

Comte's greatest conceptual error was to label his scheme a religion. Those who have given up on faith rarely feel indulgent towards this emotive word, nor are most adult, independent-minded atheists much attracted to the idea of joining a cult. That Comte was not particularly sensitive to such subtleties was made clear when he began to refer to himself as 'the Great Priest', a pronouncement which must at a stroke have wiped out his appeal among the more balanced members of his audience.

Comte's legacy, nevertheless, was his recognition that secular society requires its own institutions, ones that could take the place of religions by addressing human needs which fall outside the existing remits of politics, the family, culture and the workplace. His challenge to us lies in his suggestion that good ideas will not be able to flourish if they are always left inside books. In order to thrive, they must be supported by institutions of a kind that only religions have so far known how to build.

While no churches for the Religion of Humanity were ever built in Comte's lifetime, several decades after his death a group of Brazilian enthusiasts (one of them, as Comte himself had predicted, a wealthy banker) came together to fund the first such institution in Paris. They initially planned to erect a large edifice in the Place de la Bastille, but after reviewing the scope of their funds, they settled instead on adapting an apartment on the first floor of a building in the Marais. They hired an artist about whom history has subsequently been silent to paint portraits of the founder's secular saints and, at the front of the converted living room, an imposing neo-altarpiece of a woman and child, representing Humanity holding the Future in her arms.

Comte's secular saints included Gutenberg, Shakespeare, Descartes and the physiologist Bichat.

iii. Conclusion

1.

A central problem with any attempt to rethink some of the needs left unmet by the ebbing of religion is novelty.

Whereas we are for the most part well disposed to embrace the new in technology, when it comes to social practices, we are as deeply devoted to sticking with what we know. We are reassured by traditional ways of handling education, relationships, leisure time, ceremonies and manners. We are especially resistant to innovations which can be pegged to the thought of one person alone. To have the best chance of being taken up, ideas should seem like the product of common sense or collective wisdom rather than an innovation put forward by any single individual. What would likely be seen as a bold innovation in software can too easily, in the social sphere, come across as a cult of personality.

It is to the benefit of most religions that they have been around for many centuries, a characteristic which appeals strongly to our fondness for what we are accustomed to. We naturally defer to practices that we would reject as extraordinary if they were newly suggested to us. A few millennia can do wonders to render a fanciful idea respectable. A ritual pilgrimage to the shrine of St Anthony may be inherently no less strange, and perhaps even more irrational, than a pilgrimage around an orbital motorway, but the shrine in Padua enjoys at least one great advantage over the M25 in having been in place since the middle of the thirteenth century.

2.

Fortunately for the concepts examined here, none are new. They have existed for most of human history, only to be over-hastily sacrificed a few hundred years ago on the altar of Reason and unfairly forgotten by secular minds repelled by religious doctrines.

It has been the purpose of this book to identify some of the lessons we might retrieve from religions: how to generate feelings of community, how to promote kindness, how to cancel out the current bias towards commercial values in advertising, how to select and make use of secular saints, how to rethink the strategies of universities and our approach to cultural education, how to redesign hotels and spas, how better to acknowledge our own childlike needs, how to surrender some of our counterproductive optimism, how to achieve perspective through the sublime and the transcendent, how to reorganize museums, how to use architecture to enshrine values – and, finally, how to coalesce the scattered efforts of individuals interested in the care of souls and organize them under the aegis of institutions.

3.

It has already been conceded that a book cannot achieve very much on its own. It can, however, be a place to lay down ambitions and begin to sketch out some intellectual as well as practical trajectories. The essence of the argument presented here is that many of the problems of the modern soul can successfully be addressed by solutions put forward by religions, once these solutions have been dislodged from the supernatural structure within which they were first conceived. The wisdom of the faiths belongs to all of mankind, even the most rational among us, and deserves to be selectively reabsorbed by the supernatural's greatest enemies. Religions are intermittently too useful, effective and intelligent to be abandoned to the religious alone.

Acknowledgements

I am deeply indebted to the following for their help in the writing, thinking through or production of this book: Deirdre Jackson, Dorothy Straight, Joana Niemeyer, Richard Baker, Cecilia Mackay, Grainne Kelly, Richard Holloway, Charles Taylor, Mark Vernon, John Armstrong, James Wood, A. C. Grayling, Robert Wright, Sam Harris, Terry Eagleton, Niall Ferguson, John Gray, Lucienne Roberts, Rebecca Wright, Simon Prosser, Anna Kelly, Juliette Mitchell, Dan Frank, Nicole Aragi, Caroline Dawnay, Phil Chang and his team, Thomas Greenall, Jordan Hodgson, Nigel Coates and Charlotte, Samuel and Saul de Botton.

Picture Credits

Andrew Aitchison: 62; akg-images: 81, 116; akg-images/Stefan Drechsel: 252 (left); Alamy/ Gari Wyn Williams: 94; Archconfraternity of San Giovanni Decollato, Rome: 218 (left); Archivio Fotografico Messaggero S. Antonio Editrice/Giorgio Deganello: 126; Arktos: 250; Axiom/Timothy Allen: 24; Richard Baker: 100, 104, 146, 151, 152, 154, 157, 288; *Every Word Unmade*, 2007, by Fiona Banner, courtesy of the Artist and Frith Street Gallery, London: 214; from *Brigitte et Bernard* © Audrey Bardou: 216 (below); from *The Roman Missal, 1962* © Baronius Press, 2009: 38; Nathan Benn: 54; Jean-Christophe Benoist: 16; © Bibliothèque Nationale de France: 149; Big Pictures: 187; Bridgeman Art Library/ Bibliothèque Nationale, Paris: 302; Bridgeman/British Library, London: 72; Bridgeman/ Chiesa del Gesù, Rome: 252 (right); Bridgeman/Church of the Gesuiti, Venice/ Cameraphoto Arte Venezia: 10; Bridgeman/Duomo, Siena: 42; Bridgeman/ Fitzwilliam Museum, University of Cambridge: 141; Bridgeman/Galleria degli Uffizi, Florence: 169, 216 (above); Bridgeman/ Galleria dell' Accademia Carrara, Bergamo: 174; Bridgeman/ Hermitage, St Petersburg: 238 (below); Bridgeman/Neil Holmes: 265; Bridgeman/ © Isabella Stewart Gardner Museum, Boston: 234; Bridgeman/Musée des Beaux-Arts et d'Archéologie, Besançon/Giraudon: 223 (above); Bridgeman/Musée du Louvre, Paris/ Giraudon: 211, 232; Bridgeman/Museo di San Marco dell'Angelico, Florence/Giraudon: 236 (above); Bridgeman/Musée d'Unterlinden, Colmar: 220; Bridgeman/National Museum of Bosnia and Herzegovina, Sarajevo/Photo © Zev Radovan: 47; Bridgeman/ Noortman Master Paintings, Amsterdam: 184; Bridgeman/Prado, Madrid: 230 (above); Bridgeman/Private Collection: 118; Bridgeman/St Peter's, Vatican City: 228 (above); Bridgeman/Scrovegni Chapel, Padua: 86; by kind permission of the Syndics of Cambridge University Library: 92; Camera Press, London/Butzmann/Laif: 36; © Nicky Colton-Milne: 49; from the *Garden Ruin* series © François Coquerel: 223 (below); Corbis/Robert Mulder/Godong: 60; Corbis/Bob Sacha: 130; Jean-Pierre Dalbéra: 308, 309; Fczarnowski: 170; Peter Aprahamian/Freud Museum, London: 97 (below); Gabinetto Fotografico Nazionale, Rome: 218 (right); from the *Remember Me* series © Preston Gannaway/Concord Monitor: 228 (below); Getty Images: 236 (below), 249, 286; Thomas Greenall & Jordan Hodgson: 45, 67, 89, 97 (above), 123, 177, 193, 204–5, 226, 245, 262, 266, 274, 284, 290 (below); Dan Hagerman: 295; from *The Sunday Missal* © HarperCollins, 1984: 134; istockphoto.com: 270 (above); Rob Judges: 107; *New York*, c.1940, by Helen Levitt © Estate of Helen Levitt, courtesy Laurence Miller Gallery, New York: 230 (below); Linkimage/Gerry Johansson: 22; *Red Slate Circle*, 1987 by Richard Long. Courtesy of the Artist and Haunch of Venison, London © Richard Long. All Rights Reserved. DACS, 2010: 241 (below); Mary Evans Picture Library: 64; © Mazur/catholicchurch.org.uk: 31, 34, 40, 225 (below); © Museum of London: 270; Naoya Fujii: 260; PA Photos/AP/Bernat Armangue: 52; PA Photos/Balkis Press/Abacapress: 293; Panos Pictures/Xavier Cevera: 110; John Pitts: 270 (below); from *Contrasts*, 1841, by A.W.N. Pugin: 256; Reuters/Yannis Behrakis: 190; Reuters/STR: 297; Rex Features: 89 (inset), 144; Lucienne Roberts & David Shaw: 76, 290 (above); Scala/Art Institute of Chicago: 177 (inset); Scala/Pierpont Morgan Library, New York: 114, 128; Scala/ White Images: 238 (above); *Untitled – October 1998*, by Hannah Starkey, courtesy Maureen Paley, London: 28; Mathew Stinson: 172; *National Gallery I, London 1989* by Thomas Struth, courtesy of the artist and Marian Goodman Gallery, New York/Paris © Thomas Struth: 212; Westminster Cathedral, London: 225 (above); Katrina Wiedner: 140, 269.

Index

Also published by Hamish Hamilton and
available in Penguin Paperback

The Consolations of Philosophy

Alain de Botton has set six of the finest minds in the history of philosophy to work on the problems of everyday life. Here then are Socrates, Epicurus, Seneca, Montaigne, Schopenhauer and Nietzsche on some of the things that bother us all: lack of money, the pain of love, inadequacy, anxiety, the fear of failure and the pressure to conform.

'Few discussions on the great philosophers can have been so entertaining ... an ingenious and intelligent book' *Sunday Times*

The Art of Travel

The perfect antidote to those guides that tell us what to do when we get there, *The Art of Travel* tries to explain why we really went in the first place – and helpfully suggests how we might be happier on our journeys.

'Lucid, fluid, uplifting … it can enrich and improve your life'
Sunday Times

Status Anxiety

We all worry about what others think of us. We all long to succeed and fear failure. We all suffer – to a greater or lesser degree, usually privately and with embarrassment – from status anxiety. For the first time, Alain de Botton gives a name to this universal condition and sets out to investigate both its origins and its solutions.

'De Botton's gift is to prompt us to think about how we live and how we might change things' *The Times*

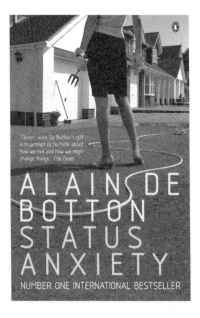

The Architecture of Happiness

The Architecture of Happiness will take you on a beguiling tour through the history and psychology of architecture and interior design, and will for ever alter your relationship with buildings. It will change the way you look at your current home – and help you make the right decisions about your next one.

'Full of splendid ideas, happily and beautifully expressed' *Independent*

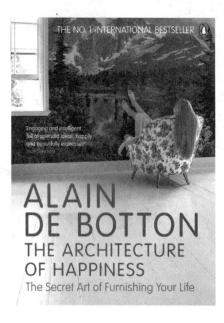